Was Called Barren

A Devotional for Women Going Through Infertility

Brandi Chase

WESTBOW
PRESS®
A DIVISION OF THOMAS NELSON
& ZONDERVAN

Scripture quotations are from the ESV® Bible (The Holy Bible, English Standard Version®), copyright © 2001 by Crossway, a publishing ministry of Good News Publishers. Used by permission. All rights reserved.

Scripture taken from The Message. Copyright © 1993, 1994, 1995, 1996, 2000, 2001, 2002. Used by permission of NavPress Publishing Group.

Scriptures marked KJV are taken from the KING JAMES VERSION (KJV): KING JAMES VERSION, public domain.

Scripture taken from the Amplified Bible, Copyright © 1954, 1958, 1962, 1964, 1965, 1987 by The Lockman Foundation. Used with permission.

This book is a work of non-fiction. Unless otherwise noted, the author and the publisher make no explicit guarantees as to the accuracy of the information contained in this book and in some cases, names of people and places have been altered to protect their privacy.

WestBow Press books may be ordered through booksellers or by contacting:

WestBow Press
A Division of Thomas Nelson & Zondervan
1663 Liberty Drive
Bloomington, IN 47403
www.westbowpress.com
1 (866) 928-1240

Because of the dynamic nature of the Internet, any web addresses or links contained in this book may have changed since publication and may no longer be valid. The views expressed in this work are solely those of the author and do not necessarily reflect the views of the publisher, and the publisher hereby disclaims any responsibility for them.

Any people depicted in stock imagery provided by Thinkstock are models, and such images are being used for illustrative purposes only. Certain stock imagery © Thinkstock.

ISBN: 978-1-5127-5881-8 (sc)
ISBN: 978-1-5127-5883-2 (hc)
ISBN: 978-1-5127-5882-5 (e)

Library of Congress Control Number: 2016916359

Print information available on the last page.

WestBow Press rev. date: 11/4/2016

Contents

Dear Friend,

I'm sitting outside on my back porch while penning a letter to you. I have an empty seat next to me, and I'm dreaming that you're sitting right next to me. It's ready for you, and I've been praying for your arrival (no pun intended).

I don't know your name. I don't know your story. But I know you're here. I know of your desire to be a mother, and I know it's not happening how you ever imagined. I know, because I've been there.

Was Called Barren was unknowingly born while my husband and I were trying to conceive our first child. During those years, I kept a journal along the way. I did not keep a journal with the intent to share my story with you. I kept a journal to keep my sanity and to cope with the feelings of hopelessness and doubt that consumed me. But God had bigger plans.

During the pregnancy of our first child, I had a prompting that I needed to start sharing our story—well, really God's story. It began by purposefully sharing a small snapshot of our fertility journey to the random ladies I would come across while running errands or when someone would want to touch my belly. And while I became more comfortable on sharing just a small snapshot, the prompting to share more of our story grew. When we started having baby showers, I felt led to share a tad bit more. And why not? I was among our close family and friends. But deep down, I knew I needed to open up even more and be really transparent about our journey.

And so here we are. I'm writing this to you, girlfriend to girlfriend. I've taken off my jewelry and let my hair down, no makeup on. I've made myself comfortable. I'm being honest with you. I've opened up and shared it all. I am being as transparent and authentic as I can be with you.

Are you ready to get real?
Are you ready to get honest and open?
Are you ready to get eyeball to eyeball and share our hearts and hurts?
Are you ready?
I am. I am ready when you are. You're not alone. I'm ready to walk through this journey with you.

Brandi

A Note from Darren Chase, Brandi's Husband

To the men, I would like to say that it was not tough on me during this time, but that would be a lie. Even though I was not going through all the hormone challenges my wife was experiencing, I was going through a mental challenge on how to comfort her. Most of the time, I would not say a word when she was telling me her struggles. Not because I did not want to but because I did not know what to say. When she would tell me that God wanted us to be fruitful and multiply, and that she was cursed because her womb was not opening, I had no response to that. I felt helpless in the infertility process and in comforting my wife. I knew that God would give us what was best for our family, and knowing that, I never felt hopeless. But I did feel helpless. So I did the only thing I knew to do. That was to pray. But I did not pray for a baby. I prayed for discernment on how to talk to my wife and tell her how God made her perfect, even though she had trouble believing it. I prayed on how to be strong for the both of us during this time of our lives. I did a lot of praying.

So in writing this letter to you, again I don't know what to say. I wish I could give you some magical answer or great advice, but I can't. All I can say is pray for God to give you the strength.

CHAPTER 1

Preparation

There was a certain man of Zorah, of the tribe of the Danites, whose name was Manoah. And his wife was barren and had no children. And the angel of the Lord appeared to the woman and said to her, "Behold, you are barren and have not borne children, but you shall conceive and bear a son. Therefore be careful and drink no wine or strong drink, and eat nothing unclean, for behold, you shall conceive and bear a son. No razor shall come upon his head, for the child shall be a Nazirite to God from the womb, and he shall begin to save Israel from the hand of the Philistines." Then the woman came and told her husband, "A man of God came to me, and his appearance was like the appearance of the angel of God, very awesome. I did not ask him where he was from, and he did not tell me his name, but he said to me, 'Behold, you shall conceive and bear a son. So then drink no wine or strong drink, and eat nothing unclean, for the child shall be a Nazirite to God from the womb to the day of his death.'" Then Manoah prayed to the Lord and said, "O Lord, please

let the man of God whom you sent come again to us and teach us what we are to do with the child who will be born."
—Judges 13:2–8

We don't know her name, but we know her as the wife of Manoah and the mother of Samson. Furthermore, we don't know much about her and her husband, except that they were obedient to the angel's commands. They didn't doubt and question if they were going to have a child but inquired on what they could learn in preparation for his birth. Their words were "Teach us what we shall do for the child who will be born."

I was discussing the books I was reading with one of my mentors a couple of years into my marriage. At the time, all I read were self-help and leadership books. Well, she had suggested adding some "fun" books and taking some time occasionally to relax. Well, I took her advice and that year added a different repertoire to my book collection. Some of them were *A Little Princess*, *Hermie: A Common Caterpillar*, *Narnia*, and *You Are Special,* to name a few. Little did I know I was starting my daughter's book collection and developing the habit to read "fun" books along with my educational books. I was preparing for being a mother.

Reflection

Ask God to reveal a characteristic, quality, or habit that He wants you to strengthen and develop (or unlearn) to prepare you for the role of being a mother.

CHAPTER 2

Praising out the Sorrows

Through him then let us continually offer up
a sacrifice of praise to God, that is, the fruit
of lips that acknowledge his name.
—Hebrews 13:15

Rejoice in the Lord always; again I will say, rejoice.
—Psalm 4:4

Make a joyful noise to the LORD, all the earth!
Serve the LORD with gladness!
Come into his presence with singing!
Know that the LORD, he is God!
It is he who made us, and we are his;
we are his people, and the sheep of his pasture.
Enter his gates with thanksgiving,
and his courts with praise!
Give thanks to him; bless his name!
For the LORD is good;

his steadfast love endures forever,
and his faithfulness to all generations.
—Psalm 100

This is the day that the LORD has made;
let us rejoice and be glad in it.
—Psalm 118:24

I remember when I was diagnosed with cervical dysplasia (abnormalities in the tissues in my cervix). My doctor referred me to a specialist at the local cancer treatment center. Just having the "c" word in the title was devastating. I had just finished my initial consultation with the specialist, and I was crying and wailing in my one-bedroom 1940s apartment. I turned on some music and blasted it as loud as it would go. It was praise and worship music, but I didn't play it to give praise and worship to God. I played it because I wanted to drown out my wailing. I didn't want to startle my neighbors, and I didn't want anyone to hear my cries. Little did I know that by hearing those words of praise and thanksgiving, my soul would be penetrated. My tears began to run dry. It was as if I was all cried out and nothing was left. There were no more tears. My intention for the praise music was to drain out the sound of my sorrow, but the praise drowned out the sorrow itself.

Reflection

Turn on some praise and worship music, and sing your praises to the Lord. When you are feeling down and out and in a funk, do the same thing—and see how it changes your spirit.

CHAPTER 3

Midnight to Morning

For his anger is but for a moment,
and his favor is for a lifetime.
Weeping may tarry for the night,
but joy comes with the morning.
—Psalm 30:5

At midnight I rise to praise you,
because of your righteous rules.
—Psalm 119:62

I rise before dawn and cry for help;
I hope in your words.
My eyes are awake before the watches of the night,
that I may meditate on your promise.
—Psalm 119:147–148

When it is dark enough, you can see the stars.
—Ralph Waldo Emerson

It is amazing what happens when reading His Word when going through "stuff." For me, God's words put things in perspective, they make things seem not as bad as I might feel that they are, and they yield hope. God gave us the gift of His Word and prayer to turn our times of desperation into relationship opportunities with Him.

One of my darkest times was after my surgery for cervical cancer. I was not sure if I was going to be able to bear children when it was all finished. From everything I had read about cervical cancer, the most common residual complication was that the cervix would not be able to hold or carry a baby for a full term. Just the possibility of that being my story frightened me. The fear got darker and darker as I waited for my follow-up appointment after the surgery. I remember when my appointment finally arrived, my first question was, "Can I have children?" When the surgeon responded, "Yes, you will be able to bear children." I quickly followed up with my next question. "Do I need to have children sooner than later?" He nonchalantly answered, "No, you don't need to rush to have children; everything is going to be fine." And I can't explain the look on his face, but his eyes had an unspoken reassurance. And in that moment, my midnight turned into morning.

Reflection

When have your days seemed like midnight?
When did God turn your midnight into day?

11

How did God turn your darkness into light?
What are the desperations you are carrying right now?
God wants to turn that desperation
into a relationship with Him.

CHAPTER 4

Building Faith

For we walk by faith, not by sight.
—2 Corinthians 5:7

So he came again to Cana in Galilee, where he had made the water wine. And at Capernaum there was an official whose son was ill. When this man heard that Jesus had come from Judea to Galilee, he went to him and asked him to come down and heal his son, for he was at the point of death. So Jesus said to him, "Unless you see signs and wonders you will not believe." The official said to him, "Sir, come down before my child dies." Jesus said to him, "Go; your son will live." The man believed the word that Jesus spoke to him and went on his way. As he was going down, his servants met him and told him that his son was recovering. So he asked them the hour when he began to get better, and they said to him, "Yesterday at the seventh hour the fever left him." The father knew that

was the hour when Jesus had said to him, "Your son will live." And he himself believed, and all his household.
—John 4:46–53

It's not what you look at that matters, it's what you see.
—Henry David Thoreau

When two of our friends were expecting their sixth child (yes, sixth child—it's not a typo), they truly believed it was a boy. I mean, as soon as they found out they were pregnant and were telling people, they didn't say, "We're pregnant," they said, "We're expecting a boy." They had not even had an ultrasound yet, but they were that certain of it. Well, when that time came to have the gender scan, guess what? It was a boy! To me, that couple was the personification of the official's faith in John 4 and what it means to walk by faith and not by sight.

Well, that wasn't me. In the area of having and bearing children, my faith became almost invisible and nonexistent. When we were expecting our first child, it didn't occur to me that I could be pregnant. I thought my iron levels were low, which was why I had been feeling so tired. When my husband brought me a home pregnancy test to take, I didn't want to take it, and I didn't believe it when it read positive with the two lines. I had him go back to the store to buy a digital test— one that would be clearer and just say yes or no. Talk about walking by sight and not by faith.

I had been discouraged because of the past disappointments. This was a drastic difference from when we started to try to have a baby. Rewind many years before when we had just moved to the suburbs, but I still had all of my doctors in the city. However, my obstetrician-gynecologist (ob-gyn) was retiring soon, and I would have to switch doctors. If I was going to have to change doctors, I figured that I might as well see what ob-gyns were in our area and see where they had hospital admitting privileges. I was so certain that we were going to have a baby soon that I went ahead and did hospital maternity tours to help narrow down my choice. Of course we were the only nonpregnant couple at the tours, but it didn't bother me one bit. I was so certain that we would have a baby soon, and I was just knocking one thing off the list before the baby was coming. I was walking by faith and not by sight.

Reflection

Do you truly believe you are walking by faith right now?
Or are you walking by sight?

Wait with expectancy. Waiting is not passive. It
is active, therefore making preparations.
Faith without actions is not faith. Put
action behind my prayers.
Move from believing to expecting.

When you get pregnant, do you know where you are going to have the baby? Do you have your doctor, midwife, or provider picked out? Walk out your faith, and take a tour of where you would like to have the baby; or schedule an interview with the provider(s) you would like to assist with the delivery of the baby.

CHAPTER 5

Vicious Cycles

Rejoice always, pray without ceasing, give
thanks in all circumstances; for this is the
will of God in Christ Jesus for you.
—1 Thessalonians 5:16–18

Not to us, O Lord, not to us, but to your name give glory,
for the sake of your steadfast love and your faithfulness!
—Psalm 115:1

In hope he believed against hope, that he should become
the father of many nations, as he had been told, "So shall
your offspring be." He did not weaken in faith when he
considered his own body, which was as good as dead
(since he was about a hundred years old), or when he
considered the barrenness of Sarah's womb. No unbelief
made him waver concerning the promise of God, but he
grew strong in his faith as he gave glory to God, fully
convinced that God was able to do what he had promised.
—Romans 4:18–21

I am encouraged from Abraham's faith, and I trust in God's promise. Paul reminds us that Abraham grew in his faith as he gave glory to God. As Abraham gave glory to God, his faith (and trust) grew as well. As I give God more glory, my faith increases in return. As my faith increases, I give glory to God. And as I glorify Him, by living for Him and believing in Him and His promises, my faith grows. This is what I call the faith-glory cycle. I have to admit; I didn't take residency on this cycle but was on a much different and vicious cycle.

When I stopped glorifying God, I allowed disbelief to grow and my faith to deteriorate. For me, glorifying God was praying for children. The more I stopped praying for children (glorifying God), the greater my disbelief grew. This continued to the point that I completely lost faith in having children, and started second-guessing if God had even promised the blessing of children.

Instead of sowing glory, and reaping faith; I sowed doubt, and reaped disbelief. If you are on the doubt-disbelief cycle, it's time to jump off and get on the faith-glory cycle.

Reflection

What does giving glory mean to you?

A habit starts with one step. It takes one step
toward creating a new habit, a habit of living in
faith and giving glory. What one step can you take
today to get back on the faith-glory cycle?

CHAPTER 6

If God Is Good, Why Is He Withholding Good?

Now to him who is able to do far more
abundantly than all that we ask or think,
according to the power at work within us
—Ephesians 3:20

For I know the plans I have for you, declares the LORD, plans
for welfare and not for evil, to give you a future and a hope.
—Jeremiah 29:11

You are the God who works wonders;
you have made known your might among the peoples.
—Psalm 77:14

For the Lord God is a sun and shield;
the Lord bestows favor and honor.
No good thing does he withhold
from those who walk uprightly.

O Lord of hosts,
blessed is the one who trusts in you!
—Psalm 84:11–12

Oh, what a promise! How I forget that He doesn't withhold good from me. In the middle of my valley, in the middle of my storm, in the middle of my struggle, right splat in the middle of it, I often forget that He does not withhold good. He is my shield, my favor. He does not withhold good from me! It's hard to remember that when you have been waiting *so long* for His goodness.

During the fertility journey, we won a vehicle. Yes, you read that correctly. We won a brand, spanking new vehicle. One of my sister's was getting married, and it happened to be the same day as an annual fundraiser that we always attended. Since we couldn't attend the fundraiser, my husband purchased raffle tickets instead. We had been saving up for a new car for me, but had decided earlier that month that we needed to postpone purchasing a car for another three months until we had saved up more money. In the meantime, though, we had been casually looking at vehicles, and red convertibles had really caught my eye. Well, we won a red Jeep in the raffle. I would count that as a red convertible! Plus, the amount of money we had saved paid for the tax, title, and license for the car. Talk about God providing! You would assume that I was super thankful, but I wasn't. Instead of having a thankful attitude, I was disgusted with God. I felt like God was playing a mean trick on me. We had been praying for a baby, not a car.

I felt like we did not need His help getting a car, but we really needed His help in supplying a baby. God was showing me how much more that He could and would do, but I missed it.

This is one of those times that I forgot what God had done, but instead solely focused on what was wrong, what hurt, and what I was currently struggling with. I dismissed what God had done for us, because it was not what I wanted or expected; however, He provided not just what we needed but also more than we could imagine.

Reflection

Write down a handful of things that God has done in your life. Don't dismiss how little or big they might seem. They are all His testimonies, and just a warm-up to what is yet to come. When you feel like God is withholding good from you, refer back to your list.

CHAPTER 7

Doing My Part

But he said to me, "My grace is sufficient for you, for my power is made perfect in weakness." Therefore I will boast all the more gladly of my weaknesses, so that the power of Christ may rest upon me. For the sake of Christ, then, I am content with weaknesses, insults, hardships, persecutions, and calamities. For when I am weak, then I am strong.
—2 Corinthians 12:9–10

And my God will supply every need of yours
according to his riches in glory in Christ Jesus.
—Philippians 4:19

I felt that I had to do "my part," which was getting my body tuned up, and then I would be ready to have a baby. Unfortunately, I did not include trusting God as part of doing my part.

When we first decided that we wanted to have a baby, I really didn't think it was a big deal to get my body ready physically.

But then, after months of this preparation, I still wasn't pregnant. I felt that all I needed was to get my body tuned up, and then "Kaboom!" It would happen. Well, it didn't quite go like that.

I got my hormone levels tested to make sure they were within normal ranges, and there turned out to be a slight imbalance. I was prescribed a low dose of compounded hormones. When I went to pick up the prescription, I was actually caught off guard. I really did not know what to expect, but I definitely wasn't expecting something that looked like a deodorant stick. Regardless, I put on the hormone cream religiously, and my hormones were balanced again, but there was still no baby. I also took an expansive blood micronutrient analysis to make sure there were not any nutritional deficiencies. I supplemented what was suboptimal, but still nothing.

Next I looked up other alternative therapies for fertility, and acupuncture was high on the list. So I looked for an acupuncturist that specialized in fertility in my area and scheduled my first session. Never in my life would I have thought I would get acupuncture. I just had weird images of people having a bunch of needles stuck in them like in the movie *Hellraiser.* I know, freakish weird, but that's the visual I had of acupuncture. Anyhow, after months of acupuncture—during which, I have to share, I got some of my best napping and relaxation ever from those sessions— still no baby.

What I initially thought was going to be a quick trip to the corner store was turning into a cross-country road trip. By correcting my imbalances and deficiencies, I strengthened my body, but I was still weak in myself. I left out the most important part of doing "my part." I was seeking to fill my own needs and perfect my weaknesses on my own, leaving God out of the equation; and ignoring Him as my ALL, my *El Shaddai*, my all-sufficient one.

Reflection

Where do you feel weak that you need His Strength?

Where do you feel insulted that you need His Strength?

Where do you feel persecuted that you need His Strength?

Where are you hardened that you need His Strength?

CHAPTER 8

When God Shows Up with Cupcakes

The steadfast love of the Lord never ceases;
his mercies never come to an end;
they are new every morning;
great is your faithfulness.
—Lamentations 3:22–23

Do not forsake me, O Lord! O my God, be not far from me!
—Psalm 38:21

It was my first appointment with the fertility specialist, and I was so nervous. For one, I did not know what to expect, but most of the uneasiness came from going alone. My husband was not able to go to the appointment, so I went by myself. The uncertainty of not knowing what to expect and facing it alone were so uncomfortable. So when I arrived to the appointment and checked-in, who did I see? I saw one of my really close friends, a comfortable face in an uncomfortable environment. I was not alone after all.

My friend was there for the same reason I was, but neither of us told the other that we were having challenges getting pregnant or that we were going to see a fertility doctor. Seeing each other was not part of the agenda, but it was part of God's. My friend waited with me until I was called in to see the doctor. And when my appointment was over and I was checking out, my friend was still there waiting for me. She smiled at me, and said, "Let's go for cupcakes!"

The last time the two of us had gone out for cupcakes, we had chatted for hours about our then-boyfriends (who were now our husbands). Cupcakes meant girl time for us! Running into her was no coincidence, and it was such a blessing. I felt like it was God telling me, "Don't worry. I'm here with you. I'm not leaving your side."

The Lord never ceases to love me, and He is always there for me and with me—and sometimes He's there with cupcakes!

Reflection

Do you feel like you are walking alone at the moment?

Where can you see God walking with you?

Where have you seen God's fingerprints in your life?

CHAPTER 9

Playing Mental Ping-Pong

Count it all joy, my brothers, when you meet trials of various kinds, for you know that the testing of your faith produces steadfastness. And let steadfastness have its full effect, that you may be perfect and complete, lacking in nothing. If any of you lacks wisdom, let him ask God, who gives generously to all without reproach, and it will be given him. But let him ask in faith, with no doubting, for the one who doubts is like a wave of the sea that is driven and tossed by the wind. For that person must not suppose that he will receive anything from the Lord; he is a double-minded man, unstable in all his ways.
—James 1:2–8

Draw near to God, and he will draw near to you. Cleanse your hands, you sinners, and purify your hearts, you double-minded.
—James 4:8

The few months when I was on the oral fertility medications were exhausting because I played mental Ping-Pong the whole time. I ping-ponged between continuing to take the fertility medications or not continuing to take the medications. My mind bounced this decision of taking or not taking them back and forth, back and forth. I felt like I had made the decision to take them, but then I would doubt my decision. I know part of the emotional instability was due to the medications themselves. I would be on an emotional high when I started the medications, along with the hopeful expectation that a baby would be coming, but then when my period would start, I would fall and fall hard. Then the mental Ping-Pong would start again about whether we would refill the prescription and start again.

When I go to the grocery store, I am adamant about not going hungry and going with a list. If I don't do these two things, I will buy things we don't need and let my emotions get in the way of my purchases. For one thing, my hunger inhibits my ability to make wise decisions, and my stomach starts leading the way. Because it is wise to make my grocery shopping decisions beforehand, deciding on what I was comfortable with in the area of the fertility medications was no different. Deciding whether or not to take the medications should have been done well before I filled the prescription. It was hard to make a confident decision during this process when I was having hormonal mood swings. I was trying to make an unemotional decision when I was very emotional. It would have been easier if I had made that decision without a doubt ahead of time, but

I was so hungry for a baby that I let my emotions lead the way and second-guessed my decisions in doing so. Despite the second-guessing every time I went to refill my prescription, I kept refilling it, month after month. But after several months of not becoming pregnant, we decided to take a break from the treatments. The mental Ping-Pong finally stopped, and I finally felt certain about our decision.

Reflection

Are there any areas that you are second guessing yourself, or being double-minded?
Write out your fertility plan that God gives you. Get specific on what you and your husband are responsible for. Pray over the fertility plan, and allow God to speak to Your Spirit on what to do. God will generously give you the needed wisdom if you ask Him for it.

CHAPTER 10

Contentment

Humble yourselves before the Lord, and he will exalt you.
—James 4:10

For everyone who exalts himself will be humbled,
and he who humbles himself will be exalted.
—Luke 14:11

I rejoiced in the Lord greatly that now at length you
have revived your concern for me. You were indeed
concerned for me, but you had no opportunity. Not
that I am speaking of being in need, for I have learned
in whatever situation I am to be content. I know how
to be brought low, and I know how to abound. In any
and every circumstance, I have learned the secret of
facing plenty and hunger, abundance and need.
—Philippians 4:10–12

I prayed for God to take the desire away to have children. I
asked for Him to settle my heart. To fill that void that I felt

from not being a mother. I wanted to be happy and satisfied with my current life, which meant not being a mother. I cannot say that I felt ashamed for not being totally content, but I felt that I should be able to get to that point of contentment.

My mother had a stillbirth when I was eight years old, my brother David. She went to the doctor because she thought she had a tumor as there was a lump on her stomach. She didn't think she was pregnant because she had monthly periods as always. But when she went to the doctor, she found out she was five to six months pregnant, but the baby didn't have a heartbeat. When I was in college, my mom told me that she understood why David didn't make it. At least for her life—that she would not have been able to take care of him and raise him. She had gotten very ill when I started college, and he would have been a preteen about that time. I don't know if that was the reason, but that was the explanation my mother had come to terms with and believed that God had her and David's best interest in mind. And He does. God has our best interests in mind, even when we don't think He does.

To me, that is coming to a place of contentment. I feel like my mom came to a place of contentment, or better yet, a point of acceptance and had come to terms with the situation. To take it a step further, I truly believe my mother came to a point of peaceful satisfaction, and that's what I desired as well. Whether I had a child or not, I wanted to be at a point of peaceful satisfaction.

Contentment leads to humility. Humility leads to contentment. I am not sure which one comes first (the chicken or egg?), but humility and contentment go hand in hand. And at this point of contentment of humbling myself, then and only then can God lift me up.

Reflection (adapted from *Brave* by Angela Thomas)
Where do you put yourself on this scale of acceptance?

ACCEPTANCE

--

--

--

COMING TO TERMS

DENIAL

What can you do today to move further
on the scale toward acceptance?

CHAPTER 11

Buying in Bulk

Moreover, it is required of stewards
that they be found faithful.
—1 Corinthians 4:2

Let every detail in your lives—words, actions,
whatever—be done in the name of the Master, Jesus,
thanking God the Father every step of the way.
—Colossians 3:17 (The Message)

Whoever can be trusted with very little can also be
trusted with much, and whoever is dishonest with
very little will also be dishonest with much. So if
you have not been trustworthy in handling worldly
wealth, who will trust you with true riches? And if
you have not been trustworthy with someone else's
property, who will give you property of your own?
—Luke 16:10–12

It came to a point where I felt that I should buy ovulation kits and pregnancy tests in bulk. I used to buy my monthly feminine products in bulk, but I stopped because every month I expected that we would get pregnant *that* month. And then whether to buy a jumbo pack of feminine products or just enough for that cycle became a mental debate for me. Same thing happened with the ovulation kits. I could buy a bonus pack (two-month supply) at a discounted rate, but then I would question, *If I do, does that mean I don't believe I'm going to get pregnant?* Everything just seemed like a challenge of should I or shouldn't I. It became a real struggle for me on being wise with finances and exercising my faith (which sounds ridiculous to me as I am sharing this).

I was oblivious to the fact that I would need the feminine products again after having a baby because I was so caught up in the now. Plus, being thrifty had nothing to do with exercising my faith. It's about being a good steward with what I've been given, and that's not elusive to finances. The time I was literally wasting by putting a question mark over everything I was doing was not being a good steward with the time God had given me.

Don't be mistaken; I totally believe that God is concerned with every area of our lives. But when it started taking me twenty minutes at the grocery store for a simple errand, I had a problem called detail-itis. I was too caught up in the penny pinching and insignificant details. There were so many more better things to do than contemplate between a regular or jumbo pack of maxi pads! God cares for me, He sees me, and He wants me to live life most abundantly. My time would have been better spent thanking God for all the provisions.

Reflection

What has God entrusted to you?

Take some time to reflect on the provisions God has provided, and thank Him for the abundance He provides.

CHAPTER 12

Living with My Blinders

Make a careful exploration of who you are and the work
you have been given, and then sink yourself into that.
Don't be impressed with yourself. Don't compare yourself
with others. Each of you must take responsibility for
doing the creative best you can with your own life.
—Galatians 6:4–5 (The Message)

And let us consider how to stir up one another to love
and good works, not neglecting to meet together, as
is the habit of some, but encouraging one another,
and all the more as you see the Day drawing near.
—Hebrews 10:24–25

Do nothing from selfish ambition or conceit, but
in humility count others more significant than
yourselves. Let each of you look not only to his own
interests, but also to the interests of others.
—Philippians 2:3–4

Behold, how good and how pleasant it is for
brethren to dwell together in unity!
—Psalm 133:1 (NKJV)

I don't know if you are like me, but I can go through a whole day and not even realize or acknowledge those around me. I get so laser focused on accomplishing things on my to-do list that I forget to stop and smell the roses and take my eyes off myself. Well, I was blessed to have someone take her eyes off herself and give me a compliment and encourage me.

It was really just an ordinary day that turned into an extraordinary evening. Some friends of ours were in urgent need of a date night, so their tween son came over after work and had dinner with us. After dinner, we all wanted some dessert, so we decided to bake a cake together, kind of like a family, and then played a card game the rest of the evening. Kind of a low-key night, but it was so much fun. So when his mom came to pick him up later that night he was telling her what we did, and she just smiled and in her Texas accent, nonchalantly said to me, "You're going to be a great mother." Now keep in mind, this is when I had given up and lost hope that I was ever going to be a mother. I felt so uneasy as she talked about my husband and I having kids. I really just could not believe it was a possibility. But as uncomfortable as it was to hear, "you're going to be a great mother," it was still encouraging to my soul. Hearing those words was like oxygen to my soul.

My friend may not even remember that night or telling me those words, but it touched my heart to the core. I am so thankful that she took her eyes off herself.

If you take your eyes off yourself and put them on someone else, something good will happen. So here are some jumpstart pointers to help you get over yourself!

1. Don't focus on yourself!
2. Put other people before yourself.
3. Work on you!
4. Sow seeds!
5. Give yourself away (it helps change your focus)!
6. Stop expecting your husband to meet all your needs; look to the Lord instead (more about this in another chapter)!

Reflection

Go to your kitchen, and grab a metal spoon out of the drawer. Face the spoon with the shallow side facing you, and look at your reflection in it. Are you facing right side up or upside down? Now take the spoon and face it outward, and look at your reflection in it. When we are facing outward, we are right side up. This is how God wants us to live our lives.

How can you focus on others?
What charity or organization can you donate some time to?
When will you start to help others?

CHAPTER 13

Crushed and Disappointed

The Lord is near to the brokenhearted
and saves the crushed in spirit.
—Psalm 34:18

Unrelenting disappointment leaves you heartsick,
but a sudden good break can turn life around.
—Proverbs 13:12 (The Message)

A joyful heart is good medicine,
but a crushed spirit dries up the bones.
—Proverbs 17:22

We had been married for four years and had been trying to conceive for almost half of our married life. So I had a conception date. You know, just like a delivery due date or a must-be-postmarked-by date. Well, I had a conception deadline, and ours was October 1. I wrote out this deadline as an affirmation, "We will conceive by October 1." Yep, I'm being totally real about this date thing; plus, I even put it in our annual goals. You might be thinking, *Why that particular date?* Well, let me tell you why. We needed a time limit—well, really needed a budget limit—on the fertility treatments. We could not afford to continue them indefinitely, and October 1 would be two years of maxing out our health care savings accounts and using all those funds exclusively for fertility treatments.

So when I say I put our conception goal date in the yearly goals, I literally added it to our spreadsheet along with all the other goals we had for that year, as if I had that much control over a goal like this. On the goal spreadsheet, the goal was typed out on the first column on the left-hand side, and each subsequent column was for writing yes or no if the goal was met. So there was a column for every month in the year; and at the beginning of each month, we would review how our monthly goals were going and what the status or progress was. So for the goal of conception, every month was "no, no, no, no, no, no, no, no, no, no, no, no."

Looking back at this, if I had to do it all over again, I would definitely not put it on my goal list. Putting it on the goal list made it seem like I had all the control over that situation; and made me focus even more on it to the point of being overly consumed with having a baby. The more I typed "no, no, no," the more crushed I became.

Reflection

When you are brokenhearted, read Psalm 34:18 out loud and reflect on the Lord's closeness in your life.

When you are disappointed, read Proverbs 17:22 out loud and reflect on the Lord's fulfillment in your life.

When you are crushed, read Proverbs 13:12 out loud and reflect on the Lord's gift of salvation.

CHAPTER 14

But God

For still the vision awaits its appointed time;
it hastens to the end—it will not lie. If
it seems slow, wait for it;
it will surely come; it will not delay.
—Habakkuk 2:3

And I am sure of this, that he who began a good work in
you will bring it to completion at the day of Jesus Christ.
—Philippians 1:6

So faith comes from hearing, and hearing
through the word of Christ.
—Romans 10:17

The same year that I had set a goal of conceiving by October 1, I had also set a goal of reading eighteen books. I had a list of books that I desired to read, but was open to adding other ones; particularly since my mentor had recommended that I add more leisure books to my reading. Well, that summer, while at a women's conference, one of the speakers talked about and recommended Max Lucado's "You Are Special." So when I went to find the book online, I could only find it in a box set with three other stories. Well, one of those stories, is now one of my favorite children's book, "Hermie: A Common Caterpillar." I love how the main character is not happy with how he is made, and is transparent with God on asking him why he doesn't have spots, or is not strong, or doesn't have a shell for a house, or other cool things like the others around him. He doesn't get mad at God, but keeps praying, and asking. When he talks to God, he feels encouraged for a little while, but then he gets discouraged again.

Through the whole story, God repeatedly tells him, "I'm not finished with you yet." I love that! I felt like God was saying that to me during my journey with fertility, but I just couldn't hear him. When the baby wave swept through my circle of friends, but skipped over me, I needed to be reminded that God wasn't finished with me yet. When one of my younger cousins, whom I remember changing her diapers when she was a baby, announced that she was expecting, I needed this reminder. Despite what your life looks like right now, the story is not over. He's not finished with you yet!

Reflection

Write down your current heartaches
and circumstances below.

_____, but God is not finished with me yet!

_____, but God is not finished with me yet!

_____, but God is not finished with me yet!

_____, but God is not finished with me yet!

Now you're not finished just yet. Speak out loud what you wrote above, including the "but God is not finished with me yet!" It is important to speak these out loud. It not only builds your faith, but it's your spiritual warfare. His word says that faith comes by hearing, and not just hearing the latest pop music jam, but by hearing His word.

CHAPTER 15

Believing for the Impossible

God can do anything, you know—far more than you could
ever imagine or guess or request in your wildest dreams!
—Ephesians 3:20 (The Message)

The Lord said, "I will surely return to you about this time
next year, and Sarah your wife shall have a son." And
Sarah was listening at the tent door behind him. Now
Abraham and Sarah were old, advanced in years. The
way of women had ceased to be with Sarah. So Sarah
laughed to herself, saying, "After I am worn out, and
my lord is old, shall I have pleasure?" The Lord said to
Abraham, "Why did Sarah laugh and say, 'Shall I indeed
bear a child, now that I am old?' Is anything too hard
for the Lord? At the appointed time I will return to you,
about this time next year, and Sarah shall have a son."
—Genesis 18:10–14

And behold, your relative Elizabeth in her old age has also conceived a son, and this is the sixth month with her who was called barren. For nothing will be impossible with God.
—Luke 1:36–37

Sarah's barrenness was gone, and Elizabeth's barrenness was referred to in the past tense. These stories really speak to me on believing God for what seems impossible. It is also comforting for me to read that Sarah laughed in unbelief that she would have children. She doubted too! I believe she wasn't much different from you and me. She wanted children, but couldn't see how.

While working with a fertility specialist, I had a laparoscopy (exploratory surgery for my uterus). My doctor found adhesions on my uterus and removed them; and also reported that I had stage-two endometriosis as well as PCOS (polycystic ovary syndrome). After the surgery, he reviewed the images he took and showed us where the adhesions were interfering with conceiving. Well, of course, he also shared that even though he removed the adhesions that there was a possibility that more could build up in the future. I remember being disheartened when looking at the images from the surgery. To physically see the roadblocks in conceiving was to me like Sarah seeing that her monthly womanly periods had ceased. After physically seeing why you cannot bear children, it's difficult to have faith that you can have children in the near future.

After the laparoscopy, we took some time off to allow my body to rest, but to also see if we could have children naturally. After a couple of months, however, disbelief started to creep in again. Below is an excerpt from my journal at this time.

Well, after the surgery, I believed that it was the start of "be fruitful and multiply" for us. I so want children, but Lord, how can that happen now? I feel so broken. I feel that if or when it's time You will make it happen. You will provide a baby. You can do more than I can imagine or think of! You are able to do something so wild and so out there, that the only explainable answer is You! Lord, I am going to leave it to You. Really, do I really have any other option? Ha! No!

Reflection

Do you believe for what's possible or for what's impossible?

Take some time and praise God for being a God
of Impossible, and for being able to do *anything*
beyond what you can think or imagine.

Read Ephesians 3:20 and Luke 1:37 out loud.

CHAPTER 16

Purity with Purpose

Flee from sexual immorality. Every other sin a
person commits is outside the body, but the sexually
immoral person sins against his own body.
—1 Corinthians 6:18

For this is the will of God, your sanctification: that you
abstain from sexual immorality; that each one of you know
how to control his own body in holiness and honor, not in
the passion of lust like the Gentiles who do not know God
—1 Thessalonians 4:3–5

But I say, walk by the Spirit, and you will
not gratify the desires of the flesh.
—Galatians 5:16

Let us walk properly as in the daytime, not in
orgies and drunkenness, not in sexual immorality
and sensuality, not in quarreling and jealousy.
—Romans 13:13

Before I got married, even before I met my husband, I took the Purity with Purpose course at my local church. The overall goal of the course is chastity and reclaiming your sexual purity. So during the course, one of our assignments was to write down boundary violations and past sexual activity. We had one week to complete the exercise, which really gave me time to recall as much as I could.

The boundary violations that I recalled included the following:

- listening to nasty or dirty jokes
- going to strip clubs or nude bars
- wearing revealing clothing and purposefully dressing a certain way to get males' attention
- flashing people and strangers
- watching sexual activity and gestures on television
- listening to music about sexual activity
- dancing dirty and provocatively
- reading magazines and books about sex or with sexual content
- looking at models, sports figures, athletes, and just men in general in a lustful manner
- allowing my thoughts to drift into daydreaming about sex

The last thing I did for the exercise was write down all my encounters with sexual promiscuity.

The next part of the exercise was to see how to protect and guard our hearts moving forward. God will protect and guard you, but we must also set boundaries to protect ourselves; as well as be mindful of our actions and behaviors. I set six boundaries that I felt would protect my heart.

The first boundary was regarding television. I didn't watch that much television at home, but when I did, it ended up being reruns of *Friends* and *Will and Grace.* So let's see, the first show was about young singles who slept around and were promiscuous. The other show was about two homosexuals and a promiscuous heterosexual roommate. I also needed to be mindful of what I watched at someone else's home, like at a family member's or friend's house. For example, I stopped by my aunt's house, and her high school daughter was watching *Desperate Housewives.* Not a good influence in this teenage girl's mind, nor for anybody else. I need to take the initiative and submit. Just turn it off, and don't try to compromise. A proactive decision I made was to purchase appropriate movies that I could watch instead of random channel surfing.

The second boundary was magazines and books. I wasn't purchasing any books or magazines, but the magazines at the hair salon would have articles on sex and also had ads for provocative clothing. My plan was to bring my own reading material, which I still do to this day.

The third boundary was to walk away from people telling dirty jokes. It's amazing how I really haven't had to exercise this boundary as my associations have changed for the better.

The next boundary was to only watch sports when there was a game I was truly interested in watching.

The fifth boundary was to dress modestly. This became easier, since I had thrown away a lot of provocative clothing. When I shop now, the clothes are more conservative.

The last boundary was to become submitted to God but also to have two or three accountability partners who I could talk to if I was struggling and with whom I could touch base when I needed.

Reflection

Take an inventory of any sexual impurity prior to marriage.

Ask God to forgive you for every area of past sexual impurity, and for the Holy Spirit to help you guard your mind and heart.

Make a plan to stay pure.

How will you keep the intimacy within your marriage?

CHAPTER 17

Mourning the Womb

to grant to those who mourn in Zion—
to give them a beautiful headdress instead of ashes,
the oil of gladness instead of mourning,
the garment of praise instead of a faint spirit;
that they may be called oaks of righteousness,
the planting of the Lord, that he may be glorified.
—Isaiah 61:3

Blessed are those who mourn, for they shall be comforted.
—Matthew 5:4

Lyrics to Nichole Nordeman's "Holy"

How many roads did I travel before I walked down one that led me to You? How many dreams did unravel before I believed in a hope that was true?

And how long? How far? What was meant to fulfill only emptied me still and all You ever wanted

Only me, on my knees Singing, Holy, holy And somehow
all that matters now is You are holy, holy

How many deaths did I die before I was awakened to
new life again? And how many half-truths did I bear
witness to 'Til the proof was disproved in the end?

And how long? How far? What was meant to illuminate,
shadowed me still And all You ever wanted

Only me, on my knees Singing, Holy, holy And somehow
all that matters now is You are holy, holy

And all I have is gratitude to offer You

You are holy, holy And somehow all that matters
now is You are holy

Only me, on my knees Singing, Holy, holy And somehow
all that matters now is You are holy, holy, holy

Holy

One afternoon while driving home from work, I was listening
to this song. This wasn't the first time I'd ever heard the song,
but this time it was so different. It was still playing when I
arrived home, and I stayed in the car until it finished. For
some particular reason, that song pierced my spirit that day.
I felt that this was what God desired of me. He desired me

to give Him everything. He wanted all of me through the barrenness. I traveled the road of barrenness, feeling empty, and mourned the death of my dream. It felt like part of me had died by not being able to bear a child. But while I mourned what I did not have, God mourned missing me. All I wanted was a baby, and all God wanted was all of me. But I was so wrapped up and consumed in what I wanted that I missed it. There was an empty hole that I thought could only be filled by having a baby, but in reality, only God could fill that hole. I needed more of Him and less of me.

Reflection

And through all of this, God is saying, all I want is you. When will you come to Me? When will you let Me fill that longing? When will you wake up to a new life? When will you die to yourself and live in Me? When will you see that all that matters is My love for you? I have an everlasting love for you; a love that never fades, never goes away, and will fill you and overflow you. When will you come to Me?

If you feel like you have not been giving God all of you, and putting your desire to have a child before Him; ask Him for forgiveness and praise Him for desiring all of you.

If you feel like you have been giving God all of you, pause and think about how He takes great delight in you and rejoices over you.

CHAPTER 18

Keeping Your Hope in Front of You

You are the light of the world. A city set on a hill cannot
be hidden. Nor do people light a lamp and put it under a
basket, but on a stand, and it gives light to all in the house.
—Matthew 5:14–15

Surely there is a future, and your hope will not be cut off.
—Proverbs 23:18

Where there is no vision, the people perish.
—Proverbs 29:18 (KJV)

We used the second bedroom in our home as an overflow
room for our clothes, Christmas decorations, and just stuff
you would normally put in an attic. We had this unspoken
expectation that it would eventually become a nursery, but
after a couple of years I started talking about making it a
prayer room. Well, to my surprise, my husband asked our
friends who are general contractors to make that dream of
having a prayer room a reality. While prepping the room for

the small remodel to happen, I unburied a lamb tummy time mat behind some furniture. I totally forgot that I even had the mat. I had purchased it about four years prior while skimming through a baby catalog and just had to have it for our future baby. Finding this perfectly wrapped mat in its original plastic wrap triggered my memory that I had wanted that room to be a nursery. For some reason, I had totally forgotten about that expectation and had unknowingly blocked it out of my memory. I took the mat out of its wrapping that weekend and hung it up in place of a window curtain. I wanted to keep it out as a visual reminder and did not want to keep my hope buried anymore.

That weekend, I was on a surprise treasure hunt for hope and didn't even know it. My hope of a nursery did not die when the bedroom was transformed to a prayer room. Instead, my hope was transformed. It transformed from the past to the future. It transformed from a noun to a verb.

Reflection

What do you want?

Do you have a visual reminder of what you want? And I'm not referring to pregnancy tests or ovulation kits. I'm talking about a baby outfit or something for the baby's room.

Get something, and keep it out where you can visually see it on a frequent basis. Don't hide it. Hiding it is hiding your dreams. Keep it as a visual reminder of God's promises for your life.

CHAPTER 19

Stinky Thinking

There was a certain man of Ramathaim-zophim of the hill country of Ephraim whose name was Elkanah the son of Jeroham, son of Elihu, son of Tohu, son of Zuph, an Ephrathite. He had two wives. The name of the one was Hannah, and the name of the other, Peninnah. And Peninnah had children, but Hannah had no children. Now this man used to go up year by year from his city to worship and to sacrifice to the LORD of hosts at Shiloh, where the two sons of Eli, Hophni and Phinehas, were priests of the LORD. On the day when Elkanah sacrificed, he would give portions to Peninnah his wife and to all her sons and daughters. But to Hannah he gave a double portion, because he loved her, though the LORD had closed her womb. And her rival used to provoke her grievously to irritate her, because the LORD had closed her womb. So it went on year by year. As often as she went up to the house of the LORD, she used to provoke her. Therefore Hannah wept and would not eat. And Elkanah, her husband, said to her, "Hannah, why do you weep? And why do you not eat? And why is your heart sad? Am I not more to you than ten sons?" After they had eaten and drunk in Shiloh, Hannah rose. Now Eli the priest was sitting on the seat beside the doorpost of the temple of the LORD. She was deeply distressed and prayed to the Lord and wept bitterly. And she vowed a vow and said, "O LORD of hosts, if you will indeed look on the affliction of your servant and remember me and not forget your servant, but will give to your servant a son, then I will give him to the LORD all the days of his life, and no razor shall touch his head."

1 Samuel 1:1–11

The heart knows its own bitterness,
and no stranger shares its joy.
Even in laughter the heart may ache,
and the end of joy may be grief.
—Proverbs 14:10, 13

By faith, Hannah conceived. Hannah wept year after year, and she was distressed year after year. Hannah cried out to God year after year and made a vow with Him, and she followed through with it.

I believed God could show up, but felt like He would not show up. It was so hard for me to understand why God had not opened up my womb. I wanted to know why. I couldn't see why He wouldn't open our womb. I cried, I wept, and I pleaded. You name it, I did it, but my womb remained closed.

I felt like I could not take much more and that something had to give. I told God that if a baby did not arrive on the scene soon, I was going to leave my husband. I started thinking that if God did not open up my womb it was His way of telling me that I should leave him and that He was not opening my womb because I was not supposed to have children with my husband. It may sound stupid, but I truly believed that if it were not supposed to be, God would block the way. I was being totally open, honest, and real with God. I really let Him know how I felt, even if it was stinky thinking.

Reflection

You heard my gabbing! I was grieving, aching, and bitter. I was having stinky thinking.

What is the aroma of your thoughts?

Are you having any stinky thoughts?

Ask God to heal your mind, and to heal your heart.

CHAPTER 20

Buried Dreams

May he grant you your heart's desire
and fulfill all your plans!
—Psalm 20:4

You have given him his heart's desire
and have not withheld the request of his lips.
—Psalm 21:2

Hold fast to dreams. For if dreams die, life is
a broken-winged bird that cannot fly.
—James Langston Hughes

It was Fourth of July weekend, and we had traveled to Colorado to visit my husband's family. It had been over a year since we had seen his nephew, and now he was walking, talking, and his cute personality was starting to come out. We had the greatest time playing with him and living in his world. That weekend reminded me of a lot of great memories I had with my family and dusted off that hidden desire to have my children grow up with their cousins. A handful of my cousins and I were all about the same age, and we had the best times growing up together. I forgot that I had always wanted my children to build those kinds of memories with their cousins also.

When we got home from our travels, I dusted off my old prayer Bible. It's really just an ordinary Bible, but it has sticky tabs on scriptures that I like to use for prayers. I opened it to the book of Luke and looked at the battered and worn-out tab that said "my children." Well before I was even married, I had been praying Luke 2:40 for over a decade—that my children will grow and become strong, be filled with God's wisdom, and His grace will be upon them.

I prayed that verse again that day, and continued to. I slowly started believing again that God knew the desires of my heart, and that He would grant them.

Reflection

God knows the desires of your heart, including your desire for children. Believe that He'll grant them, and stretch yourself and start thinking of the hopes, wishes, and dreams you have for your children. God cares about every detail of your life.

Lift up those dreams, hopes, and wishes you have for your children to God, and thank God in advance for them.

CHAPTER 21

Who Do You Seek First?

When Rachel saw that she bore Jacob no
children, she envied her sister. She said to
Jacob, "Give me children, or I shall die!"
—Genesis 30:1

Then God remembered Rachel, and God
listened to her and opened her womb.
—Genesis 30:22

I cry out to God Most High, to God who
fulfills his purpose for me.
—Psalm 57:2

My soul, wait silently for God alone, for
my expectation is from Him.
—Psalm 62:5 (NKJV)

> With my voice I cry out to the Lord; with my
> voice I plead for mercy to the Lord.
> —Psalm 142:1

Rachel should have cried out to God, not to her husband about her barrenness. That really spoke to me. I should have shut my lips when I wanted to complain or whine about not having children to my husband and go to God instead. God is first, even before my husband. My three takeaways from Rachel were that she compared herself, she cried to her husband instead of God, and she was envious (but we'll talk about that later).

Even though Rachel cried out to her husband, God still remembered her. Do you realize that? God *remembered* her! God didn't cast her off. God did not push her to the back burner, like she did to Him. God did not take revenge, or treat her how she treated Him. That's the mighty and sovereign God we serve. He puts us first, even when we don't put Him first. He opened her womb.

I remember there was a time that I dreamed and wished of being able to have a miscarriage. I know, that sounds morbid, but I'm being honest with you. At that moment, I so desired to just know that I could bear a child or get pregnant, that it would be a victory. Oh, what little faith I had. I was so desperate! I really truly thought that if I had a miscarriage, at least I would know that I could get pregnant. I wasn't thinking about the hurt that I would feel, or the pain from the loss. Oh, how much I was shortchanging what God could do and would do. Thank God he didn't answer that prayer, but that's where I was at one point. I felt like Rachel, that I would rather die if I couldn't have a baby. That's all I wanted … I just wanted a baby.

Reflection

Take some time right now, and pray to God.
Physically get on your knees, and cry out to Him.
Confess any times that you went to your husband
or another person instead of seeking Him first.
Praise God for who He is, and for being always merciful.
Cry out to him the desires of your heart.

CHAPTER 22

Thought Life

Rejoice in the Lord always; again I will say, rejoice. Let
your reasonableness be known to everyone. The Lord
is at hand; do not be anxious about anything, but in
everything by prayer and supplication with thanksgiving
let your requests be made known to God. And the
peace of God, which surpasses all understanding, will
guard your hearts and your minds in Christ Jesus.
Finally, brothers, whatever is true, whatever is honorable,
whatever is just, whatever is pure, whatever is lovely,
whatever is commendable, if there is any excellence, if there
is anything worthy of praise, think about these things.
—Philippians 4:4–8

I was sitting at the computer typing some things at the office,
and the song "Remember When" came on by Alan Jackson.
The lyrics triggered my mind to wonder if I ever was going to
have those life moments he sung about in the song. My mind
thought, *What if I never know what it's like to be a parent,
an empty nester, or a grandparent?* I didn't realize what was

happening until the keyboard was kissed with my tears. At that moment, I caught my thoughts and stood up to change the music.

You have to first decide to take control of your thoughts. And once you've made up your mind, you have to do it one thought at a time. Once you've been able to become aware of when you're having these thoughts, what to do to replace them comes next. Make your brain and mind like a sponge for God's Word; so that you can replace those negative thoughts with God's truth. And if you have a negative thought (well, really, when you catch yourself in a negative thought), you have a choice to make. Yes, it is all a choice!

I know this is easier said than done. I really had to work on my emotions and fight the battle with my mind, and I'm still walking through that battle today. It's an active process in taking your thoughts captive. Put those thoughts on trial, and compare them to what God says. When we're familiar with God's truth, we can literally challenge any comment, trigger, or thought with the following questions:

- Is it true?
- Is it beneficial?
- Is it necessary?

If the answer is no, then we don't need to open the door of our hearts and minds to it. We can take the power within us to walk away from that thought and all the negativity it could harvest.

Reflection

Compare your mind to a kitchen pantry.
What are you stocking the shelves with?
Are there items that need to be discarded?
Are there some that can stay?

When you get a negative thought this week,
pause and challenge it with God's Word.
Look up Scriptures that speak what is true and right.

CHAPTER 23

What Schedule?

The plans of the heart belong to man,
but the answer of the tongue is from the Lord.
All the ways of a man are pure in his own eyes,
but the Lord weighs the spirit.
Commit your work to the Lord,
and your plans will be established.
—Proverbs 16:1–3

Many are the plans in the mind of a man,
but it is the purpose of the Lord that will stand.
—Proverbs 19:21

There cannot be a crisis next week.
My schedule is already full.
—Henry A. Kissinger

I like order. I like schedules. I like planning. I work well with a calendar. But the fertility treatments are a whole other level of planning, that I would consider it the opposite of planning when you get down to the core of it. It's more like craziness—the craziness of dropping everything and going to the doctor for an ultrasound, the craziness of feeling like a pushpin from all the testing, and the craziness from all of the medications.

When you urinate on the ovulation kits at home, it's recommended that you use the second urination of the day and complete it before 9:00 a.m. The timing of the second urination was so stressful to me. I needed to wake up earlier than usual so that I could make it to work on time if it were a positive reading. And if the ovulation test showed a smiley face (positive reading), I would call the doctor's office to schedule an ultrasound and blood work for that same day. And dependent on the results, we would go in the next day for an intrauterine insemination (IUI). So when all of this happens, all plans get thrown out the window, and everything revolves around the insemination.

For me, that meant urinating a second time early enough to let my vanpool now that I wouldn't be carpooling but also have enough time to get to work since I wasn't going to be in the high-occupancy vehicle (HOV) lane. I didn't share what was going on with anyone, and that included the people I vanpooled with, so I couldn't even pick up another rider to ride with me so I could get in the HOV lane. And not sharing with any of them was silly. There were eight people on my vanpool, and all but two were Christians. I could have had some stress relief, and six other believers praying for me.

Plus trying to get whatever work I needed to get done that day, all while going to the doctor's office for an ultrasound during my lunch break, was pretty stressful in itself. And then after work, prior to the fertility treatments, I would go for a jog at the end of the workday if I were not on my vanpool, which would let me avoid rush hour traffic. But when you're ovulating and trying to get pregnant, it's recommended to take it easy that week. So instead of going for a jog, I would sit in more traffic and be more stressed after a long day. I was totally living against myself.

Below is what a day might look like during the IUI process.

5:45 a.m.—wake up, immediately urinate, and drink a huge glass of water

6:05 a.m.—jump in the shower, and drink another huge glass of water

6:20 a.m.— get out of shower and urinate on an ovulation test

6:21 a.m.—contact vanpoolers that I won't be riding and get dressed like a mad woman

6:30 a.m.—coffee is ready (hopefully if I remembered to set it the night before); make mocha and pack my lunch

6:40 a.m.—drive to work with my fists clinched on the steering wheel

6:41 a.m.—turn on the radio to hear traffic updates and pray that there are no accidents on my route

7:05 a.m.—reach the toll way and call the doctor's to schedule an ultrasound

8:05 a.m. (hopefully)—arrive at work

11:30 a.m.—use my lunch break to get ultrasound and blood work

12:20 p.m.—arrive back at work, scarf down my lunch, and finish rest of workday

Reflection

Challenge: One day this week, don't schedule anything, don't look at a calendar, and live in the moment.

Bonus
Don't wear a watch or look at a clock during the day.

CHAPTER 24

Be a Sunflower

But the fruit of the Spirit is love, joy, peace, patience,
kindness, goodness, faithfulness, gentleness, self-
control; against such things there is no law.
—Galatians 5:22–23

We plant seeds that will flower as results in our lives,
so best to remove the weeds of anger, avarice, envy and
doubt, that peace and abundance may manifest for all.
—Dorothy Day

We've all heard the phrase, "Bloom where you're planted."
Well, I believe that phrase more and more every day, and I like
to put a twist on it. Sunflowers bloom where they're planted.
When I think of sunflowers, I not only think of summer, but
I also instantly admire their beauty of radiant yellow and
gold colors as well as their height that makes them stand out
so boldly. There is a lot more to sunflowers than their outer
beauty. They have a lot of internal toughness. Sunflowers are
hearty, tough flowers that can grow and be beautiful in poor

soil, extreme heat, and little rain. Plus, despite their growing conditions, they always turn toward the sun.

I feel that you and I are like sunflowers. Even though there may not be a child growing in me at the moment, I can still be cheerful, inviting, and beautiful like a sunflower and be able to resist the dry, hot, and severe conditions. Plus, I can turn toward God like a sunflower, and bloom where I'm planted.

Reflection

To me, a sunflower is the embodiment of the fruit of the Spirit. Draw a nine-petal sunflower. Write your name in the middle part of it, and then write each fruit of the Spirit in the petals.

Bonus

Pick up a sunflower at the floral shop, or if they're not in season yet, get a picture of one, and place it where you can see it throughout the week. Every time you look at the sunflower, be encouraged to look toward God and be reminded that you are beautiful, cheerful, and inviting.

CHAPTER 25

2 > 1 or Two Are Better than One

Two are better than one, because they
have a good reward for their toil.
For if they fall, one will lift up his fellow. But woe to
him who is alone when he falls and has not another to
lift him up! Again, if two lie together, they keep warm,
but how can one keep warm alone? And though a
man might prevail against one who is alone, two will
withstand him—a threefold cord is not quickly broken.
—Ecclesiastes 4:9–12

You use steel to sharpen steel, and
one friend sharpens another.
—Proverbs 27:17 (The Message)

I had heard so many times not to speak about something until
it's a victory. I believe I took that a little too literally. I foolishly
listened to the devil's lies on not calling on other believers to
stand in the gap for me, to hold my hand with me, to not go

through it alone. I needed the protection in the area of my mind and thoughts.

I did not share with my inner circle that we were going through fertility treatments. Wait, I need to rephrase that sentence. I did not share with *anyone* that we were going through fertility treatments. I didn't want anyone to know. I tried to hide it. I felt like less than a woman. I felt ashamed.

But someone did reach out to me. She saw it in my demeanor; she noticed the ups and downs, the uneasiness, and the restlessness. We worked together and were next-door office mates.

I praise God for her. She took me aside and genuinely asked me if everything was all right. She was His hands and feet. She had me relax and take a breather in her office and sat next to me, hands enclosed mine, and prayed with me. No judgment on my tears, just prayed with me. It's amazing how much peace I felt after that moment and how my vulnerability brought comfort. How tired I had become from living under a veneer.

Reflection

Go to your front door, and look how small the hinges
are in comparison to the height and weight of the
door. Count the number of hinges on the door. Little

hinges swing big doors. Life swings more easily to and fro with three hinges—God, a friend, and me.

Do you have a third hinge (female friend) swinging life with you? If the answer is yes, reach out to her, and thank her for lifting you up and swinging life together. If the answer is no, ask God who that person is, and reach out to them to start swinging life with them.

CHAPTER 26

Birth Control

And God blessed them. And God said to them,
"Be fruitful and multiply and fill the earth and
subdue it, and have dominion over the fish of the
sea and over the birds of the heavens and over
every living thing that moves on the earth."
—Genesis 1:28

Have mercy on me, O God,
according to your steadfast love; according
to your abundant mercy
blot out my transgressions.
Wash me thoroughly from my iniquity,
and cleanse me from my sin!
For I know my transgressions,
and my sin is ever before me.
Against you, you only, have I sinned
and done what is evil in your sight, so that
you may be justified in your words
and blameless in your judgment.

Behold, I was brought forth in iniquity,
and in sin did my mother conceive me.
Behold, you delight in truth in the inward being,
and you teach me wisdom in the secret heart.
Purge me with hyssop, and I shall be clean;
wash me, and I shall be whiter than snow.
Let me hear joy and gladness;
let the bones that you have broken rejoice.
Hide your face from my sins,
and blot out all my iniquities.
Create in me a clean heart, O God,
and renew a right spirit within me.
Cast me not away from your presence,
and take not your Holy Spirit from me.
Restore to me the joy of your salvation,
and uphold me with a willing spirit.
Then I will teach transgressors your ways,
and sinners will return to you.
Deliver me from blood guiltiness, O God,
O God of my salvation,
and my tongue will sing aloud of your righteousness.
O Lord, open my lips, and my mouth declare your praise.
For you will not delight in sacrifice, or I would give it;
you will not be pleased with a burnt offering.
The sacrifices of God are a broken spirit;
a broken and contrite heart, O God, you will not despise.
—Psalm 51:1–14

> So if you are presenting your offering at the altar, and while
> there you remember that your brother has something
> [such as a grievance or legitimate complaint] against
> you, leave your offering there at the altar and go.
> First make peace with your brother, and
> then come and present your offering.
> —Matthew 5:23–24 (AMP)

When I am going through a struggle and am up at midnight or the wee hours of the morning, I am not giving praise to God. I am usually asking for help. Also, in my prayer life, I feel like I do not give enough praise and that I am usually asking for things that I want or need. When I look at my prayer habit in relation to the ACTS (adoration, confession, thanksgiving, and supplication) method, I often hang out in supplication. It is so rare, almost to the point of nonexistence, that I give adoration, confession, or thanksgiving. Well, I usually do give thanksgiving at mealtime prayers for our food, the provisions, and the relationships and lives that are represented at that meal, but usually that is the only time.

I remember when I was a practicing Catholic and would take time to review my life, particularly my sins, before going to confession and made it a habit to participate in reconciliation. The sacrament of reconciliation is when you go to a priest, confess any sins you have committed, and ask for forgiveness. I still believe that confession is an important habit to have, but to physically go to that person I've wronged (if applicable) and confess to them directly instead of a priest.

One night I woke from my sleep at about 3:00 a.m., and I was thinking about a baby and if there was any sin hindering that in my life. I went *way* back and dug deep. Birth control. Birth control kept popping up. Birth control. There it was again: birth control became the dominant thought and answer I received that morning.

I started birth control when I was eighteen years of age. I really don't remember how it was all orchestrated, but it was my freshman year of college, and all my friends were on birth control. I had never had a gynecological appointment, and I remember taking one of my friends to her appointment at the local free clinic, so I made an appointment also. I started on birth control that day and was on some sort of birth control for the next seven years.

God has called us to be fruitful and multiply. Birth control limits childbirth and reproduction, and is not in line with God's will for our lives. Until that night, I really didn't see anything wrong or sinful about taking birth control. I realized that I was acting against God's will and plan for my life to be fruitful and multiply. I was taking things into my own hands and working against His promises. I confessed to God and was truly remorseful for what I had done. Since taking birth control was not something so out there or blatantly wrong, I hadn't even realized it was sin.

Reflection

Take some time to pray using the ACTS method.

Adore God for who He is, and for His
unfailing and unending mercies.
Confess any sin, especially in the area of
limiting or preventing pregnancy.
Thank God for washing you clean, white as snow.
Supplicate and humbly ask God for what's on your heart.

CHAPTER 27

Baby Promises

By the God of your father who will help you,
by the Almighty who will bless you
with blessings of heaven above,
blessings of the deep that crouches beneath,
blessings of the breasts and of the womb.
—Genesis 49:25

He will love you, bless you, and multiply you. He will
also bless the fruit of your womb and the fruit of your
ground, your grain and your wine and your oil, the
increase of your herds and the young of your flock, in the
land that he swore to your fathers to give you. You shall
be blessed above all peoples. There shall not be male or
female barren among you or among your livestock.
—Deuteronomy 7:13–14

May God be gracious to us and bless us and
make his face to shine upon us, *Selah*

that your way may be known on earth, your
saving power among all nations.
Let the peoples praise you, O God; let
all the peoples praise you!
Let the nations be glad and sing for joy, for you judge the
peoples with equity and guide the nations upon earth. *Selah*
Let the peoples praise you, O God; let
all the peoples praise you!
The earth has yielded its increase;
God, our God, shall bless us.
God shall bless us; let all the ends of the earth fear him!
—Psalm 67

He gives the barren woman a home,
making her the joyous mother of children. Praise the Lord!
—Psalm 113:9

Behold, children are a heritage from the Lord,
the fruit of the womb a reward.
Like arrows in the hand of a warrior
are the children of one's youth.
Blessed is the man who fills his quiver with them!
He shall not be put to shame
when he speaks with his enemies in the gate.
—Psalm 127:3–5

Your wife will be like a fruitful vine within your house
—Psalm 128:3

I urinated on the ovulation stick, and it was a happy face, which meant I was ovulating, but my husband was in Portland, Oregon, for a work conference. He still talks about that trip, more because of the fun he had and how weird the people were. However, I remember that weekend too, but not for the same reasons. I wanted a child so bad, and this was going to be our first intrauterine insemination (IUI), but he wasn't there. I remember that evening, I drew a bubble bath; and the jets actually worked (they never had worked previously). And I was just relaxed, and was not really stressed out, frustrated, or disappointed, but instead I was hopeful that we would have another try at it the next month.

[Below are a couple of excerpts from my journal during the IUI process.]

August 27

Today is the day. It's four days after my birthday, and we are receiving a second IUI. God has a chosen time for my prayers to be answered, for His mission to be accomplished, and for miracles to take place. When I get pregnant, I need to remember that God did not forget me, but will I remember to give Him the glory?

If it's through intrauterine insemination, can I really say it was God? Well, since the first insemination didn't work, but if it works this time, God be the glory!

September 8

I just realized not being pregnant right now is the "desire of my heart." The desire of my heart is to be a full-time, stay-at-home mother. My efforts should not be on trying to get pregnant. It will happen at the right time. My focus should be on staying home full time, and when that happens, I'll become a mother.

September 15

We are headed to the Bahamas to celebrate our wedding anniversary. This is such a perfectly timed get away, even though we didn't plan it that way. It has been so stressful these past couple of weeks, leading up to the IUI yesterday.

September 27

Our third IUI failed. I have a follow-up appointment with our fertility doctor to discuss our options. I am tired of expecting and hoping but then every month being reminded that it didn't happen again. After two years of trying to have a baby, this is getting pretty depressing. I am tired. I want to believe that I will get pregnant, but it is getting harder and harder to believe. I am tired of the calendar day counting, the ovulation kits, the ultrasounds, the IUIs, and the pregnancy tests, just all of it. This is not fun and romantic!

Reflection

When you dreamed of having a baby, did you ever envision
that it would require so many tests and pre-prenatal
appointments? How did you envision having a baby?

However you dreamed of having a baby, reflect
back on the fact that God is faithful and He
will bless your womb and your house.

Reread God's promises; and believe these
promises for you and your husband.
Genesis 49:25
Deuteronomy 7:13–14
Psalm 67
Psalm 113:9
Psalm 127:3–5
Psalm 128:3

CHAPTER 28

Suddenlys

Unrelenting disappointment leaves you heartsick,
but a sudden good break can turn life around.
—Proverbs 13:12 (The Message)

And suddenly there came from heaven a sound
like a mighty rushing wind, and it filled the
entire house where they were sitting.
—Acts 2:2

About that time Herod the king laid violent hands on some
who belonged to the church. He killed James the brother of
John with the sword, and when he saw that it pleased the
Jews, he proceeded to arrest Peter also. This was during
the days of Unleavened Bread. And when he had seized him,
he put him in prison, delivering him over to four squads
of soldiers to guard him, intending after the Passover to
bring him out to the people. So Peter was kept in prison,
but earnest prayer for him was made to God by the church.
Now when Herod was about to bring him out, on that very

night, Peter was sleeping between two soldiers, bound with
two chains, and sentries before the door were guarding
the prison. And behold, an angel of the Lord stood next
to him, and a light shone in the cell. He struck Peter on
the side and woke him, saying, "Get up quickly." And the
chains fell off his hands. And the angel said to him, "Dress
yourself and put on your sandals." And he did so. And he
said to him, "Wrap your cloak around you and follow me."
And he went out and followed him. He did not know that
what was being done by the angel was real, but thought he
was seeing a vision. When they had passed the first and the
second guard, they came to the iron gate leading into the
city. It opened for them of its own accord, and they went
out and went along one street, and immediately the angel
left him. When Peter came to himself, he said, "Now I am
sure that the Lord has sent his angel and rescued me from
the hand of Herod and from all that the Jewish people were
expecting. "When he realized this, he went to the house
of Mary, the mother of John whose other name was Mark,
where many were gathered together and were praying. And
when he knocked at the door of the gateway, a servant girl
named Rhoda came to answer. Recognizing Peter's voice,
in her joy she did not open the gate but ran in and reported
that Peter was standing at the gate. They said to her, "You
are out of your mind." But she kept insisting that it was so,
and they kept saying, "It is his angel!" But Peter continued
knocking, and when they opened, they saw him and were
amazed. But motioning to them with his hand to be silent,
he described to them how the Lord had brought him out of

the prison. And he said, "Tell these things to James and to the brothers." Then he departed and went to another place.
—Acts 12:1–16

And suddenly—oh, how I love those two words! The story in Acts 12 is a "And suddenly" story to me. I just love what happens when Rhoda answers the door. She was so surprised that Peter was at the door that she forgot to open it. God is a God of suddenlys! The people were praying for Peter to be released but then were amazed when he showed up at the door. This story just fires me up! Please walk through it with me.

In verse 5, the church gathered together for fervent prayer to God for Peter. They gathered together, and stood in the gap for Peter.

Then in verses 7 and 23, God changed the circumstances *quickly* and *suddenly*. In verses 11 and 17, God intercedes and performed miracles; plus Peter acknowledged it was God's deliverance. Then in verse 15, the people couldn't believe that their prayers were answered! What they persistently prayed for was answered. Then in verse 16, when Peter was finally let in, the people's shock and surprise changed to excitement!

I was so tired of the endless pattern: hope that I would get pregnant, and then my period would start ... and repeat. The hope of getting pregnant consumed my every thought. I was not able to think clearly, and my everyday life started to be completely wrapped up with having a baby. So after three failed IUI treatments, we decided to take a break from the treatments. We still wanted to get pregnant, but we wanted to just try on our own. We continued to test my ovulation status, but that was it. Being totally consumed with having a baby didn't go way, but it definitely decreased significantly.

I would pray for children, pray over the fertility medications, pray before and after every doctor appointment, and pray before and after every insemination, but then I would still have doubts of my "suddenly."

At the time, I felt like I was the only person going through this and feeling this way, but in hindsight, I know there were and are other women going through a similar rollercoaster ride of waiting for our "suddenlys." So to let you know that you're not alone, I included excerpts from my journal during the first couple months after we stopped fertility treatments.

Month 1

Last night when I took the ovulation test, it was a smiling face! Oh, I want to *believe!* I really want to believe that we're going to get pregnant now. Part of my brain wants to revert to the things of the past, but I don't want to think on negative stuff. Lord, I desire that You hear and heard my cries, and answer me. We had sex earlier this morning, but after the ovulation test, we did it again at night. In all honesty, we probably would not have had sex again, but we did "for good measure." Lord, all I know is that if—or maybe I should say *when*—we get pregnant, it's all You. No question, no doubt.

Month 2

This hurts. I took a pregnancy test, and it was negative. Again. As always.

Month 3

I am scared. I am scared to speak negatively. I want to buy a pregnancy test, but I decided against it. My period is usually every twenty-one days, but I'll wait until Monday. If it's not here by Monday, then I'll buy a pregnancy test because that will be a full twenty-eight days. To take it a step further, [my friend] kept talking about us needing a baby, and her wishing for one. And so I waited until Wednesday, a full thirty days. And my period started. It started *immediately* after I took the pregnancy test. My husband stayed with me after I took the test while we waited for the results. I did cry a little later in the morning, but not uncontrollably.

Month 4

So today is day 35. I want to buy a pregnancy test, but then I don't because of what happened last month. Immediately, I mean immediately, after I took the pregnancy test last month, my period started. I'm trying to think the longest my period was late but I really can't remember. Last month, I think it was twenty-nine days. Lord, I don't want to be anxious. I so want to believe that I am pregnant.

Next Day

And my period started *again.*

I really wanted to believe there was a "suddenly" right around the corner. I wanted to have faith that I was going to get pregnant ... *suddenly.* But I was tired. I was tired of waiting for my suddenly.

God is a God of suddenlys and can change things in a blink of an eye. We need to get excited with expectancy and not be shocked or surprised when God shows up! But we also must not lose hope of our suddenly.

Reflection

Think about the church in Acts 12. Are you opening the door of your answered prayers with shock and disbelief; or are you having trouble opening the door because of your overwhelming excitement?

What "suddenlys" have you seen in your life?

Praise God for being a God of suddenlys. Praise Him for your past suddenlys, and for your suddenlys yet to come.

CHAPTER 29

Being Called or Driven

Trust in the Lord with all your heart,
and do not lean on your own understanding.
In all your ways acknowledge him,
and he will make straight your paths.
—Proverbs 3:5–6

For God is not a God of confusion but of peace.
—1 Corinthians 14:33

And let the peace of Christ rule in your hearts, to which
indeed you were called in one body. And be thankful.
—Colossians 3:15

After we went through what seemed like an eternity of fertility treatments, we started exploring the option of adoption. It felt that we were giving up if we opted for adoption, but at the same time we didn't want to lose out on an opportunity to start a family.

We went to one informational meeting with a local adoption agency, but soon after we heard the founder of a ministry we supported guest speak at a local church, and we were reminded that they also facilitated adoptions. We felt that if we chose the adoption route, it would be through that ministry that we had supported for many years. Before the ministry founder was introduced, there was an introduction and testimonies shared of how two families were impacted by her ministry. There were two sets of twins adopted by two different families at that church. One of those families was the worship leader, and she shared her testimony about infertility and adoption that evening. During her testimony, she also had a slideshow that started with a picture of her and her husband, and then the pictures transformed from couple's photos to family photos. Oh, how I wished our photos would transform from a couple's photo shoot to a family photo shoot.

So after that evening, we started the adoption process. We had completed all the applications, questionnaires, surveys, and even had our criminal background checks. The only thing left was getting a social worker for our home study. Once we got to this point, we had some major life changes happen and decided to pause the application process. But after that, when adoption did come up in conversation, it always turned into an ugly snowball of hurt feelings and heated emotions.

My husband and I were not on the same page about adoption. When we talked about adoption, it was not easy, it was uncomfortable, and it was frustrating. Just the fact that we couldn't see eye to eye on adoption should have been a hint that it would not be our route to starting a family.

In the back of my mind, I had always thought that someday I would adopt a child. But it was never a desire to do that before having my own children. It was something I thought would happen after having my own children. But when we had a less than speedy pregnancy, it seemed like adoption became more of an option. I always thought I would choose adoption because I wanted to, not because I had to; which is where I felt that we were. We were in the "have to" not "want to," which is not the best place to be. I believe that it should be "want to" and "get to," not "have to"!

We felt like we were being driven but not called to adoption. Being called is being led by God, and being driven is being led by our own fleshly desires. We were not being called to adoption. We were driven. So after some heavy conversations, we decided not to revisit the adoption process. No adoption for our family, at least at that point in our lives.

Reflection

Evaluate your motives. Are you being called or driven?

Ask God for revelation and peace regarding
the growth of your family.

CHAPTER 30

Stupid Things People Say

Hatred stirs up strife,
but love covers all offenses.
—Proverbs 10:12

Overlook an offense and bond a friendship;
fasten on to a slight and—good-bye, friend!
—Proverbs 17:9 (The Message)

Good sense makes one slow to anger,
and it is his glory to overlook an offense.
—Proverbs 19:11

"When you stop trying, you'll get pregnant."

"Just relax, then you'll get pregnant."

"Stop trying, and then you'll get pregnant."

"Plan a big trip, and then you'll get pregnant."

"Adopt, and then you'll get pregnant. I had a friend of my neighbor's fifth cousin's uncle removed that adopted and then got pregnant."

"Stop running marathons, then you'll get pregnant."

"If you adopt, you won't have to lose your body figure."

"I thought you would be pregnant by now."

Do any of these lines sound familiar? You probably can add more to my list, but seriously, isn't it crazy what people will say? Actually, I just think they don't know what to say. They feel sorry for you and the situation and want to say something but are not really sure what. Unfortunately, more times than not, what they say is pretty harsh even when that's not the intent. They mean well, and they want to be comforting, but it comes across as being hurtful.

The worst thing we could do is take offense. Taking offense is a choice.

We disrupt the relationship when we take offense. We're better off rebuking the offense and moving on. Offense has a small root. If we water and feed the offense, it will grow, but if we starve it, it will die.

Reflection

Are there any offenses that you have
allowed its root to grow?

Are there any well-meaning friends or family members that
have said some less than helpful things during this time?

Ask God to give you the love to wash away the offense. If
you feel led, share with them in love your thoughts on their
response and suggestions for more encouraging words.

If someone tells you something "ridiculous,"
meditate on the study verses from this chapter.

CHAPTER 31

Making a Way in the Desert

Remember not the former things,
nor consider the things of old.
Behold, I am doing a new thing;
now it springs forth, do you not perceive it?
I will make a way in the wilderness
and rivers in the desert.
—Isaiah 43:18, 19

This is my commandment, that you love
one another as I have loved you.
—John 15:12

Whoever conceals his transgressions will not prosper, but
he who confesses and forsakes them will obtain mercy.
—Proverbs 28:13

Do not be conformed to this world, but be
transformed by the renewal of your mind, that by

testing you may discern what is the will of God,
what is good and acceptable and perfect.
—Romans 12:2

It was a beautiful day. Not too hot for Texas, but just right. I was relaxing and lying in our hammock on the back porch, waiting for my husband to get home from work. I had a pretty full day, which consisted of shopping at the lingerie boutique for some new undergarments to wear that night to surprise my husband. I was looking forward to celebrating that we had only one more step to complete before submitting our application for adoption. Well, the evening did not go as I was planning. That evening when my husband came home, he confessed his sins of watching pornography and committing adultery.

We immediately paused the adoption process, and my desire to have children temporarily vanished. For forty days after his confession, we slept in separate beds and did not have any physical sexual contact. We lived as roommates.

My husband immediately started individual counseling, and six months later I started group counseling. I recovered with prayer and counseling; and focused on working on myself. I learned to find my identity in Christ. I learned to seek my approval from God, and not from my husband or anybody or anything else. I cannot say that I have completely healed from this yet, but my heart is being mended everyday.

The evening of my husband's confession, I sent a group text message to five friends who I knew would cover me with prayer. I didn't mention any details in the text but simply asked for them to pray for me. When my long-time friend from childhood called to check in on me, I could not talk. My mouth was moving, but my voice was muted. She just knew what to say, and she knew what to share. Her parents, whom I looked up to dearly and adored, who loved me like their own when I was with them, dealt with infidelity and recovered from it. Just knowing that their marriage was made whole, renewed, and restored to so much led to my decision to stay in my marriage.

As a Christian, I believe I am supposed to forgive and love unconditionally in the same way God loves me and has forgiven me—even when it hurts, and even when it's my husband who hurt me. How could I say I love like Jesus if I automatically chose to walk away from my marriage? When I wanted to push the divorce button, I thought of my friend's parents, and of how Jesus faithfully and unconditionally loves and forgives me.

Staying in my marriage was the hardest decision of my life. I decided that divorcing him was a cop out, and that it was the easiest thing to do but not the best thing. I felt like I had every reason to leave biblically, but I chose to stay.

His confession was the end of one chapter but the beginning of another. There was healing that started with that confession and breakthrough in the area of our barrenness. About nine months after his confession, my husband shared that he now had an overwhelming desire to have children. About that time, my desire to have children had returned as well. For the first time, we both were on the same page of wanting children.

Reflection

Is there any sin in your life? Is there any division in your marriage? Is there any division in any of your relationships?

Take some time to pray and reflect on the above questions. Thank God for the power of the Holy Spirit, and ask Him to reveal anything that needs to be exposed in your life and relationships. Lastly, thank Him for renewed strength in trusting His will for your life.

CHAPTER 32

Baby Showers

A friend loves at all times
—Proverbs 17:17

And let us not grow weary of doing good, for in due
season we will reap, if we do not give up. So then, as
we have opportunity, let us do good to everyone, and
especially to those who are of the household of faith.
—Galatians 6:9–10

An attitude of gratitude brings opportunities.
—Unknown

I really did not understand how to handle baby showers, so
I just avoided them all together. I know, pretty cowardly, but
that was my coping mechanism. In hindsight, I feel that it
would have been best if I didn't avoid them but was open
and transparent about what was going on. I was so happy
for my friends that were expecting and loved how God was

blessing them, but mixed with my joy was sadness that I wasn't pregnant like they were.

When one of my best friends and I were in high school, she would talk about us growing up and having kids at the same time. It was just one of those childhood dreams we had. Well, when that season of our life came, I did not go to any of her baby showers. She has three children, and I did not go to a single one of the showers. And when she had her first son, my parents visited them at the hospital, but I only sent flowers.

I was excited for the arrival of their little bundle of joy. I truly was happy and excited for her, but I had a hard time showing it. I wanted to love and support her, but I had to do it from a distance. It's not that I loved her less; it was just hard for me to show it.

Love your friends the best you can. They will still love you; especially if they truly are your friends. Likewise, if you truly are their friend, you can love them at all times.

Reflection

Praise God for another's blessing(s) because it gives you a hint to what is coming your way.

CHAPTER 33

Mirror, Mirror

The Lord your God is in your midst,
a mighty one who will save; he will
rejoice over you with gladness;
he will quiet you by his love; he will
exult over you with loud singing.
—Zephaniah 3:17

I praise you, for I am fearfully and wonderfully made.
Wonderful are your works; my soul knows it very well.
—Psalm 139:14

No longer do I call you servants, for the servant
does not know what his master is doing; but I
have called you friends, for all that I have heard
from my Father I have made known to you.
—John 15:15

You have not chosen Me, but I have chosen you and I
have appointed and placed and purposefully planted

you, so that you would go and bear fruit and keep
on bearing, and that your fruit will remain and be
lasting, so that whatever you ask of the Father in My
name [as My representative] He may give to you
—John 15:16 (AMP)

for the Father himself loves you, because you have
loved me and have believed that I came from God.
—John 16:27

Every time I would go to the OB/GYN's office for my annual checkups, it seemed as if every single one of her pregnant patients had an appointment the same day and same time I did. Or one time when we were flying back from Colorado, and it appeared to be a pregnant lady convention at the airport. It just seemed as if pregnant women were surrounding me. When I would see someone pregnant, I would have a rainbow of emotions.

I felt insecure.
I felt like an outcast.
I felt not good enough.
I felt damaged.
I felt incomplete.
I felt sad.
I felt broken.

Part of these feelings stemmed from me basing my self-image on my mother status. Plus, I was also outwardly and superficially comparing myself to others.

My self-image and identity should *not* wrapped up in the following:

- my ability to have children
- my husband
- my occupation
- the size of my house or the car that I drive
- the clothes that I wear
- the bling on my finger
- where I vacation

This list can go on and on, but you get the idea. Our worth and value should be based on God, and not on anything else. Our identity and self-image is based upon the truth that we are created in the image of God.

Furthermore, when I am down on myself, or am having less than positive thoughts about myself, I have to get *prozactive*! *Prozactive* means getting proactive in cheering myself up.

What that looks like for me is taking a jog outside, allowing myself an afternoon slumber on the couch or on the porch, reading God's word, praying to God, taking a bubble bath, practicing yoga, having a girls day or night out, getting some quiet time alone to journal, lighting scented candles, or having fresh flowers in the house.

You are good enough. You are not damaged. You are complete. You are created in the image of God.

Reflection

You are God's Delight!

Grab a handheld or vanity mirror, and
tell yourself these reminders:
He made me wonderfully (Psalm 139:14).
He calls me friend (John 15:15).
He rejoices over me (Zephaniah 3:17).
He chose me (John 15:16).
He loves me (John 16:27).

CHAPTER 34

Why Is She Pregnant and I'm Not?

A tranquil heart gives life to the flesh,
but envy makes the bones rot.
—Proverbs 14:30

Let not your heart envy sinners, but continue
in the fear of the Lord all the day.
—Proverbs 23:17

Love is patient and kind; love does not
envy or boast; it is not arrogant
or rude. It does not insist on its own way; it is
not irritable or resentful; it does not rejoice at
wrongdoing, but rejoices with the truth.
—1 Corinthians 13:4–6

Let us not become conceited, provoking
one another, envying one another.
—Galatians 5:26

One morning at the office, one of the young ladies who was working a short-term contract for us shared that she was one month pregnant. I was a tad shocked since this would be her second child out of wedlock. I wasn't sure what I should say or if I should even say anything at all, but with my best poker face, I told her congratulations.

I kind of felt like I was lying or internally backstabbing her. On the outside, I pretended that I was happy for her, but on the inside I was furious. I just couldn't believe that with all of her circumstances God opened her womb. She was not married, had little to no financial means to pay for the baby (she had applied for food stamps and Medicaid), and she was scared to tell her parents (whom she lived with). I kept asking myself, "Why her? Why not me?"

When she shared her fears on why she was scared to tell her parents, for fear of their shame, I had a choice to make. I could express my frustration and jealousy and really share what I was thinking on the inside, or I could pour out encouragement, love, and grace as Jesus would. I would like to say that I did just that and never mentioned a negative word about it again, but I didn't. To her face, I would shower her with supportive and encouraging words with a fake smile. However, in the privacy of my own home, I would let the fire loose and vent like no tomorrow to my husband. It was so hard for me to show her grace. Grace is not being judgmental. Grace is not comparing. Grace is not being envious or jealous. I had to fake it until I made it. In other words, my heart had to catch up to my head.

There was another time that God gave me the opportunity to walk through envy and jealousy. It was around Valentine's Day, and one my friends shared that her oldest daughter was expecting. My first thought was, "Really, another teenage pregnancy?" My friend had been a pregnant teen when she was in high school, and now her daughter was a pregnant teen. Neither of them was married, and I was jealous that God had opened their wombs. What I believed to be a generational curse was starting to look like a generational blessing. It just didn't seem fair. I felt like God was continually blessing their wombs with children out of wedlock. I knew that I shouldn't be jealous, but it was so hard not to be. But then I heard the "love" scriptures for the umpteenth time. For some reason it seemed to relate with the uneasiness I was having regarding unplanned and teenage pregnancies. I know that it was no coincidence, but it was God's doing to help me change my focus, to be happy for her and not jealous. It reminded me that it was not about me or what I thought. It reminded me that God is our mediator, and He was asking me to do my part by showing love to her. It literally took everything in me to express joy in this situation instead of envy and jealousy.

Reflection

Have you been comparing yourself to another?

Have you been envious or jealous of another's situation?

Pray out loud that you are love as
described in 1 Corinthians 13.

I am love.
I am patient.
I am kind.
I am not envious or boastful.
I am not arrogant or rude.
I do not insist on my own way.
I am not irritable or resentful.
I do not rejoice with wrongdoing, but rejoices with the truth.
I am love.

CHAPTER 35

Date Night

Hannah's husband asked her, "Why do you weep? Why is
your heart sad? Am I not more to you than ten sons?"
—1 Samuel 1:8

from men by your hand, O Lord,
from men of the world whose portion is in this life.
You fill their womb with treasure;
they are satisfied with children,
and they leave their abundance to their infants.
As for me, I shall behold your face in righteousness;
when I awake, I shall be satisfied with your likeness.
—Psalm 17:14–15

Now the Lord God said, "It is not good (beneficial)
for the man to be alone; I will make him a helper
[one who balances him—a counterpart who
is] suitable and complementary for him."
—Genesis 2:18 (AMP)

> But I want you to understand that the head of
> every man is Christ, the head of a wife is her
> husband, and the head of Christ is God.
> —1 Corinthians 11:3

> However, each man among you [without exception] is to
> love his wife as his very own self [with behavior worthy of
> respect and esteem, always seeking the best for her with an
> attitude of lovingkindness], and the wife [must see to it] that
> she respects *and* delights in her husband [that she notices
> him and prefers him and treats him with loving concern,
> treasuring him, honoring him, and holding him dear].
> —Ephesians 5:33 (AMP)

My behavior communicated that I was not satisfied with my husband. My behavior also spoke that I loved him less than I wanted a child. My actions communicated that having a child was more important to me than he was. I got so worked up and focused on trying to have a child that I forgot that my spouse was a gift. I forgot to appreciate my husband, but at the same time, I also forgot that he was not my everything. Before trying to have a child I had made him my everything, and then as we were trying to have a baby, conceiving became my everything. My priorities were totally out of whack. I should have put God first, husband second, and conceiving last. I am sharing this not to tell you what to do or how to feel, but to share that the way I did it didn't go so well. I felt that if I had my priorities rearranged as God first, husband second, and children third, life would have been much smoother.

My husband made it a point to ensure we had date night every week, and I completely did not appreciate it. At the time, I neither understood the value of date night or his effort in expressing his love to me. And our date nights were not just dinner and a movie or something easy, but he would really take the time and effort to plan something fun, special, and exciting for both of us.

In the midst of fertility treatments, which seemed like a full time job, I would get so overwhelmed and overloaded that I wouldn't want to go on a date with my husband. I was so emotionally exhausted that taking a nap sounded so much more appealing than a night out. Well, one evening after work, my husband surprised me and took me to the Cirque Du Soleil show that was in town. I went, dragging my feet, but I am so glad he made me go. The show was *awesome*! The energy from the stage being centered at the bottom of the big top tent, and the gymnastics and athleticism were amazing! I am glad my husband bought the tickets and took me on a "not our usual" date.

That night, I was reminded of how much I enjoyed spending time with him and remembered why I married him. It's like I fell in love again that night.

Now, I'm not sharing all this to get lovey-dovey and brag on my husband. I'm sharing this so that someone else hopefully doesn't make my same mistakes. My prayer for you is to not be so tired, overwhelmed, and overloaded that you stop enjoying the now. We can't enjoy tomorrow. We can only enjoy the now.

Reflection

Plan a spontaneous date night with your husband. It doesn't have to be super elaborate or expensive; just something quirky and fun that both of you would enjoy. The goal is to reconnect with each other, and have fun with each other!

CHAPTER 36

Control Freak!

Now Sarai, Abram's wife, had borne him no children. She had a female Egyptian servant whose name was Hagar. And Sarai said to Abram, "Behold now, the Lord has prevented me from bearing children. Go in to my servant; it may be that I shall obtain children by her." And Abram listened to the voice of Sarai. So, after Abram had lived ten years in the land of Canaan, Sarai, Abram's wife, took Hagar the Egyptian, her servant, and gave her to Abram her husband as a wife. And he went in to Hagar, and she conceived. And when she saw that she had conceived, she looked with contempt on her mistress. And Sarai said to Abram, "May the wrong done to me be on you! I gave my servant to your embrace, and when she saw that she had conceived, she looked on me with contempt. May the Lord judge between you and me!" But Abram said to Sarai, "Behold, your servant is in your power; do to her as you please." Then Sarai dealt harshly with her, and she fled from her.

—Genesis 16:1–6

And God said to Abraham, "As for Sarai your wife, you
shall not call her name Sarai, but Sarah shall be her name.
I will bless her, and moreover, I will give you a son by her.
I will bless her, and she shall become nations; kings of
peoples shall come from her." Then Abraham fell on his
face and laughed and said to himself, "Shall a child be born
to a man who is a hundred years old? Shall Sarah, who is
ninety years old, bear a child?" And Abraham said to God,
"Oh that Ishmael might live before you!" God said, "No,
but Sarah your wife shall bear you a son, and you shall
call his name Isaac. I will establish my covenant with him
as an everlasting covenant for his offspring after him. As
for Ishmael, I have heard you; behold, I have blessed him
and will make him fruitful and multiply him greatly. He
shall father twelve princes, and I will make him into a
great nation. But I will establish my covenant with Isaac,
whom Sarah shall bear to you at this time next year."
—Genesis 17:15–21

Trust in the LORD with all your heart,
and do not lean on your own understanding.
In all your ways acknowledge him,
and he will make straight your paths.
—Proverbs 3:5–6

The more I tried to control, the more I felt out of control.
When looking at Sarai's fertility journey, I see myself in some
ways. I felt like I was trying to have children by any means
possible; like Sarai.

Some of the characteristics of Sarai that spoke to me were:

- Lacked patience to trust God to keep His promise
- Looked to her own methods
- Attempted to fulfill God's will in her way
- Impatience and desire for control
- Tried to make things happen her way (and by her timetable)
- Depended on her own strength instead of God's strength
- Worked independently of God

My all time low through this journey was when I asked my doctor about going through a medically induced menopause or having a partial hysterectomy. My rationale (or really my excuse) was that my periods were getting bad again (it had been a couple years since the laparoscopy), and since I believed that it wasn't in God's plans for me to have a child, why bear with that discomfort? Plus, my periods were just another reminder of not being able to have a child. Yep, it was pretty cowardly. When I told my husband about the conversation I had with my doctor, he finally broke down. He was at his wit's end of trying to convince me or show me that I was not allowing God to be in control. He shared that I was taking things into my own hands and taking away the possibility of being called "mommy" but also for him to be called "daddy."

I didn't want to pull a "Sarai"—meaning not following God, but doing my own thing, and falsely convincing myself that it is of God.

The fact that I really did not have control over the whole situation really messed with me. I literally hated that no matter what I chose to do, God was the one ultimately in control.

Reflection

What steps or actions have you done, trying to control the situation and doing everything in your means?

What step can you take today to let it go, and trust in Him to do what is His will for your life and His timing?

Are you trying to walk in your own power?
Are you moving out of God's grace and provision?
Where are you relying on your own understanding instead of wholeheartedly trusting in God?

CHAPTER 37

Take the Desire Away

Know therefore that the Lord your God is God, the
faithful God who keeps covenant and steadfast
love with those who love him and keep his
commandments, to a thousand generations
—Deuteronomy 7:9

Therefore do not throw away your confidence,
which has a great reward. For you have need of
endurance, so that when you have done the will
of God you may receive what is promised.
—Hebrews 10:35–36

And now I am about to go the way of all the earth,
and you know in your hearts and souls, all of you, that
not one word has failed of all the good things that
the Lord your God promised concerning you. All have
come to pass for you; not one of them has failed.
—Joshua 23:14

Every word of God proves true; he is a shield
to those who take refuge in him.
—Proverbs 30:5

May he grant you your heart's desire
and fulfill all your plans!
—Psalm 20:4

God always does what he says, and is
gracious in everything he does.
—Psalm 145:13 (The Message)

Children were a desire of my heart. The dream of my heart was not to just be a mother but also to be a stay-at-home mother. My husband and I had been working toward me being able to stay home when our first child was born. After three years of working with that end in mind, I was able to walk away from full-time employment. However, that was only half of the dream; we were missing the child(ren).

Only receiving half of the promise did not add up to me. Something was missing from the equation. God never goes bad on His promises. I knew that God's word *always* stayed true, and that His word *never* expires or goes void. So if children were the desire of my heart, and He grants our heart's desires, then something had to give, and I knew it had to be me.

I cried out to God to make the desire of children go away. If it was not His heart's desire for me, I begged Him to take it away. And that was my prayer.

Reflection

Let's pray together.

Lord, You know the desires of my heart, and Your Word says that You will fulfill all my plans and grant my heart's desire. Let Your heart's desire become my heart's desire. Your Will not mine, Lord. Let Your Will be done.
In Jesus's mighty name, amen.

CHAPTER 38

Deferring Life

For everything there is a season, and a time
for every matter under heaven:
a time to be born, and a time to die; a time to
plant, and a time to pluck up what is planted;
a time to kill, and a time to heal; a time to
break down, and a time to build up;
a time to weep, and a time to laugh; a time
to mourn, and a time to dance;
a time to cast away stones, and a time to
gather stones together; a time to embrace,
and a time to refrain from embracing;
a time to seek, and a time to lose; a time
to keep, and a time to cast away;
a time to tear, and a time to sew; a time to
keep silence, and a time to speak;
a time to love, and a time to hate; a time
for war, and a time for peace.

He has made everything beautiful in its time. Also, he has put eternity into man's heart, yet so that he cannot find out what God has done from the beginning to the end.
—Ecclesiastes 3:1–8, 11

Every promise of God proves true;
he protects everyone who runs to him for help.
—Proverbs 30:5 (The Message)

Take as a gift whatever the day brings forth...
—Horace

I had just finished running my first half and full marathons when we had first started trying to have a baby. I was on a runners' high, eager to sign up for more races, but I felt like I shouldn't sign up for more because I might get pregnant or I might be pregnant when the race arrived. Well, after a couple of years of not getting pregnant, I finally signed up for another full marathon. It was when I finally gave up and said, if I get pregnant, I get pregnant. If I don't, I don't. If I have to defer, I can defer. Well, registration for Marine Corps Marathon was upon us, and that was one of the marathons on my bucket list. It was actually the only marathon I really wanted to do when I started endurance running. So I booked our lodging for that trip, since we were going to make it a family vacation. My father in law is a Vietnam veteran whom served in the US Marines; and it's been one of my husband's dreams to be able to visit Washington, DC, with his father. So we figured, we could do it all in one trip. So two weeks before registration opened up, we found out we were pregnant. Imagine that. I kept postponing running a marathon, and when I finally said forget it and didn't think we were ever going to get pregnant, we ended up pregnant. In addition, the estimated due date for our first daughter was two weeks after the marathon. On a side note, I ran in a small veteran's day run four days before our first daughter was born. Oh, how God is faithful!

There is a time and season for everything. We don't know the time or day when our promise will be answered, but don't put your life on hold. Live by faith, knowing that His promise will prove true.

Reflection

Have you paused living your life?

Is there something in your life that you have been deferring?

How can you live your life to the fullest, living out your faith that there is a season for everything?

CHAPTER 39

Watch Your Mouth

The mouth of the righteous is a fountain of life,
but the mouth of the wicked conceals violence.
—Proverbs 10:11

On the lips of him who has understanding, wisdom is found,
but a rod is for the back of him who lacks sense.
—Proverbs 10:13

The wise lay up knowledge,
but the mouth of a fool brings ruin near.
—Proverbs 10:14

When words are many, transgression is not lacking,
but whoever restrains his lips is prudent.
The tongue of the righteous is choice silver;
the heart of the wicked is of little worth.
—Proverbs 10:19–21

The mouth of the righteous brings forth wisdom,
but the perverse tongue will be cut off.
The lips of the righteous know what is acceptable,
but the mouth of the wicked, what is perverse.
—Proverbs 10:31–32

A fool's mouth is his ruin,
and his lips are a snare to his soul.
—Proverbs 18:7

From the fruit of a man's mouth his stomach is satisfied;
he is satisfied by the yield of his lips.
Death and life are in the power of the tongue,
and those who love it will eat its fruits.
—Proverbs 18:20–21

As we look not to the things that are seen but to the things that are unseen. For the things that are seen are transient, but the things that are unseen are eternal.
—2 Corinthians 4:18

Now faith is the assurance of things hoped
for, the conviction of things not seen.
—Hebrews 11:1

As we are walking through the fertility journey again, I have to catch my words when people ask how many children we have. When I respond, "We have one right now;" the usual reply I get is, "Oh, she's an only child." I nicely respond, "No, she's going to be a big sister someday. She's our first child, but she will not be our only child." Or if they ask if we want more children or if we're trying to have children right now. My usual response is "We're not *not* trying." But then they respond, "Yeah, if it happens, it happens." And no, it's not "if it happens, it happens." It's "When it happens, it will happen."

When someone asks you if you have any children, instead of saying, "No, we don't have any children," can I suggest that you say, "We don't have any children *yet.*" Or when you're introduced as a young couple without kids, nicely respond, "Yes, we are a young couple, but we'll be having a quiver full of kids in the near future." It may seem awkward at first, but feel strengthened in knowing that there is power in your words. The words that come out of our mouths produce images inside of us—in our spirit and in our mind. Those images produced inside of us from our mouths, will be manifested in the seen. As Christians, and the power of the Holy Spirit, our words have the power of God accompanying them. Call things that are not, as though they already are. Speak what you want, not what you have. Whatever you believe is true; and whatever you allow to occupy your mind will sooner or later determine your words and actions.

Reflection

Using God's truth, make an affirmation card
of what is not seen *yet*. Verbally speak out
your affirmation in front of a mirror.

Below are a couple of sample affirmations
to help you get started.

I, <u>(insert your name)</u>, am a joyful mother
of children (Psalm 113:9).

<u>(Insert your husband's name)</u> and I are blessed above all
peoples, and will not be barren. We will have a quiver
full of children (Deuteronomy 7:14, Psalm 127:4–5).

I, <u>(insert your name)</u>, am a fruitful vine, and will have
a table surrounded by joyful children (Psalm 128:3).

CHAPTER 40

Comforting When You Need Comforting

Blessed be the God and Father of our Lord Jesus Christ, the Father of mercies and God of all comfort, who comforts us in all our affliction, so that we may be able to comfort those who are in any affliction, with the comfort with which we ourselves are comforted by God. For as we share abundantly in Christ's sufferings, so through Christ we share abundantly in comfort too. If we are afflicted, it is for your comfort and salvation; and if we are comforted, it is for your comfort, which you experience when you patiently endure the same sufferings that we suffer.
—2 Corinthians 1:3–6

So I was training for my first half marathon after having our first child, and it was challenging to say the least. I was not very motivated to get my long runs in, and I was having difficulty staying consistent with the training. I was thankful that I had a group of ladies to run with on Saturday mornings, but it still was challenging. They hit the pavement at the crack of dawn, which meant setting an alarm clock to wake up in the morning. It's really not that big of a deal, I was just not very motivated and preferred to wake up to my internal alarm clock. In all honesty, any excuse not to run worked for me. So when it was time to do eight miles, I ran with the group of ladies, and it seemed effortless. When that same distance was on my plan a couple of weeks later, I didn't run with the group but ran by myself. Well, I ended up running back home halfway and didn't finish all the mileage. I know the difference between the two runs—one was with others, and the other was alone. God made us for community, and living in community with others makes all the difference.

When I was going through fertility treatments, I didn't tell anyone, but I should have. At least it would have helped to keep my head clear, but also to have others stand in the gap and pray on my behalf. It just would have made going the distance more bearable.

Well, after that half marathon I was training for, we hung out in the VIP tent and made some new friends. There was one couple we just seemed to hit it off with, and our daughter seemed to get attached to the wife pretty easily. We really connected with them, and somehow I ended up sharing our journey of infertility. By the time we said good-bye and parted ways, the wife shared that she and her husband were trying to have a baby and had just seen a fertility specialist. We've been able to keep in touch since the race, and it is such a blessing and honor to be able to pray for her, encourage her, and walk alongside her in prayer through her journey.

God comforts us so that we can comfort others. Keep praying for people and sharing your testimony; you just never know who you will comfort and how God will use you.

Reflection

What can you do today to take your eyes off of yourself? Is there someone in your life that you can encourage and give a verbal compliment? Can you pray for someone; give a call to an old friend; or send a birthday card to a loved one? What can you do?

Who will you share your journey with? I recommend someone that will pray with and for you.

Printed in the United States
By Bookmasters